HUMAN CAPITAL SUPPLY CHAINS

Thanks for teaching
us at the Staffing
Executive Session.

Tim Guldd
3/10

HUMAN CAPITAL SUPPLY CHAINS

Tim Giehll and Sara Moss

Mill City Press, Inc.
212 3rd Avenue North, Suite 290
Minneapolis, MN 55401
612.455.2294
www.millcitypublishing.com

ISBN - 978-1-934938-77-5
ISBN - 1-934938-77-7
LCCN - 2009937906

Cover Design and Typeset by Jenni Wheeler

Printed in the United States of America

We dedicate this book to our families, coworkers, and employers who have supported our efforts to bring attention to this critical business issue.

We are grateful to the practitioners and academic experts who have offered their input and insights.

In subsequent editions, we will include more examples, success stories, and case studies from our readers. We invite you to share your feedback and human capital supply chain experiences on our website:

www.humancapitalsupplychains.com.

Table of Contents

Preface

Corporate leaders who can react quickly to market changes are strategically positioned to hire the best and most qualified people more readily than their competition. We believe there is a way for companies of any size to decrease their total cost of "human" capital while maintaining or increasing their overall workforce quality.

Our message is intended to be useful for:

- executives of corporations looking for new ways to drive costs out of their business while gaining competitive advantage;

- heads of procurement who want to better manage their company's total cost of human capital;

- human resources (HR) and recruitment leaders who want to hone their staffing practices to improve business performance;

- staffing firms, consultancies, and outsourcers who are looking to develop strategic relationships with their clients and increase the value they add to their clients;

- software vendors and third-party service providers interested to know how their offerings fit into the emerging human capital supply chain.

We define the "human capital supply chain" as the business processes, technology, and organizations responsible for planning, hiring, onboarding, and offboarding (processes of hiring and terminating employees) a company's human capital. Human capital supply chains link business strategy, business performance, strategic workforce planning, and staffing for improved corporate financial management and greater business success.

"Human capital" is an umbrella term that refers to all of the people that provide services and work products to an organization. Human capital includes: part- and full-time employees, independent contractors, consultants, business services providers, and outsourcers.

While we chose the term human capital, we considered alternative synonyms such as person, laborer, worker, employee, resource, and talent. Talent is the most commonly used term, but generally refers to an existing individual employee, which is too limiting for our purposes. We ask corporations to apply supply chain concepts more holistically and consider *all* of the types of human capital they use.

Workforce analysis and management almost always focuses on permanent, full-time workers. However, this internal workforce represents a shrinking portion of a company's human capital because the use of outside workers, especially temps and outsourcers, is on the rise. Executive management often lacks visibility into the total cost of human capital.

Human resources experts have encouraged corporate leaders to pay more attention to engaging and retaining their workforce for decades. We recommend that leaders apply more personal attention to optimizing their workforce for another very rational reason. In our knowledge economy, the workforce is the highest operating expense, so reducing the total cost of human capital is arguably the best way to decrease overall operating costs and increase long-term profits.

Starting in the 1980s, applying supply chain management concepts to manufacturing and other industries resulted in a reduction in the cost of goods and services produced while also increasing quality. Applying supply chain management concepts and skills to optimize human capital is an obvious idea. Yet, little has been written around the topic, making it difficult to understand how companies might actually apply these concepts to improve business performance.

We hope to provide business leaders with a deeper and more detailed understanding of key human capital supply chain concepts, along with the motivation to achieve the potential benefits when launching programs that manage human capital supply chains.

Human capital supply chain leaders, such as Hewlett-Packard and IBM, are continuously improving several human capital supply chain areas. Optimizing each area of the supply chain certainly yields benefits, but it is equally important to look at the supply chain as a whole to ensure that problems and costs aren't merely pushed to another part of the chain. This approach enables additional gains to be achieved from improving the whole system and achieving a synergy between the parts.

After decades of experience as industry generalists, working with manufacturing organizations and consulting to large staffing and recruiting companies, we have become increasingly intrigued in recent years with the potential of human capital supply chains. We offer these concepts and ideas as the start of a new conversation in the industry.

Chapter 1: The Human Capital Supply Chain

If you hire, onboard, manage, and pay your workers, then by definition, you already have a human capital supply chain (HCSC). You may have a variety of outside talent, like temps, contractors, and consultants, and/or you may outsource entire business functions to specialist organizations (called business process outsourcing or BPO). Further, you likely have established processes for assessing the performance of your talent, methods for improving performance, and processes for offboarding talent that might not be effectively meeting your needs. If only managing a HCSC were simple and straightforward!

If you have limited visibility into your total cost of human capital and your workforce planning and management is siloed (works in isolation with little interaction with other departments in the organization), you can be missing out on millions or even billions of cost savings by not managing your HCSC in a holistic way and paying attention to the entire HCSC — not just its parts. A formalized human capital supply chain management (HCSCM) program will yield rewards.

The CEO Must Demand Total Visibility

In most companies, the permanent or direct workforce is managed out of one department (HR) and the indirect or flexible workforce (e.g. temps) is managed out of another (procurement). The management of professional service engagements is most likely handled by line managers and executives. Even the smallest of firms utilizes third parties to provide legal, accounting, or marketing services, which are at the discretion of line managers in keeping with their budgets. If an organization is large or complex, there may be multiple HR, procurement, and business units involved, each of which may define much of their own processes. In most large companies, the HCSC crosses all aspects of the organization; but roles, responsibilities, and expectations are unclear and unorganized. More importantly, it is almost impossible to calculate the total "spend" (cost outlay) on human capital because each department may track human capital expenses differently.

A critical issue is that most companies don't bother trying to understand the total cost of their human capital. With partial visibility into the costs along with certain blind spots, this can mean a huge amount of unmanaged expense. Most firms focus on managing the compensation and benefit costs of their permanent workforce and leave the management of indirect workforce costs to procurement or hiring managers. Indirect and direct workforce costs are usually spread out and managed in isolation (siloed). Frequently tradeoffs are made between worker types (e.g. temp versus permanent worker), or full-time employees and contractors both work together to deliver the same project. Managing direct and indirect labor costs in two, separate buckets makes absolutely no sense. These human capital cost management responsibilities need to be integrated. The CEO must bridge the organizational silos and demand a unified view and the holistic management of the company's total spend on human capital.

Billion Dollar Benefits

Human capital supply chain management is a new concept, so it is impossible to estimate how much money can be saved. In the first decade of the new century, vendor management systems (VMS) brought about a savings of five to twenty percent on the cost of temporary labor within the first year of their implementation (primarily through vendor consolidation and rate management). It is realistic to assume that a similar savings could be garnered across all worker types. For a Fortune 500 firm, we can estimate that a holistic HCSCM program could drive out a few billion dollars in savings.

The biggest hurdle to implementing a holistic HCSC management program is the cost and complexity of tying together the technology that automates the entire HCSCM process. HCSCs connect a variety of technologies that cross organizations, business units, and suppliers. Additional costs include: developing new business capabilities like strategic workforce planning, human capital performance measurement, and the change management costs of pulling onboard the diverse stakeholders and participants.

The business rationale and the high-level return on investment (ROI) for implementing a HCSCM program are compelling.

You are not Starting from Scratch

While HCSC concepts are new, most manufacturing supply chain concepts can be applied to the HCSC.

In the last quarter of the twentieth century, a transformation occurred that took us from a manufacturing economy to a knowledge economy. For most companies, human capital became not only the largest expense, but also the most important asset.

It's time to refocus the lessons learned optimizing product lines and apply them to optimizing the workforce. The supply chain management discipline has expanded from manufacturing to accommodate a wide range of industries, including retail, entertainment, and electronic products and services. There are many methodologies, tools, and concepts that can easily be applied to the HCSC.

Those in HR, procurement, staffing, and the executive suite are aware that typically there are massive and costly inefficiencies throughout the workforce planning and hiring processes. Everyone wants a cost-effective, quality-oriented staffing process, but most firms have a limited idea about how to refine their practices to hire the right type of talent with the right skills, at the right place, at the right time, at the optimal price.

If the cost savings upside is massive and the risk of change is low because existing corporate knowledge can be applied, why aren't HCSCM programs commonplace?

HR vs. Procurement

From the HR point of view, people are "human beings." To say that may sound obvious, but HR leaders often fear that "human capital supply chain" sounds a bit too much like an assembly line. Even the term "human capital" is seen as a cold label that somehow minimizes the "human." HR personnel are frequently concerned that the organization will overdevelop the analytical and scientific approach to human capital management, somehow equating people to widgets.

Those in procurement have the opposite concern. Quite at home with widgets, procurement leaders are often uncomfortable with the complexities, "messiness," and emotions involved in hiring people.

Establishing a HCSC requires HR and procurement to put aside their fears and sensitivities. HR must trust that the organization is not going to treat people as widgets, which would not be a sound long-term management practice anyway. Procurement must recognize that they can leverage their goods procurement experience, but must also adjust their approach to address the uniqueness of people and teams. Each group must understand that it makes good business sense to apply the same sound financial management to the planning and procurement of the workforce as they do in all of the other aspects of the business.

Start Speaking the Same Language

Successful HCSC programs are reliant upon hiring managers, HR, procurement, and staffing suppliers all working in concert with a shared set of goals and objectives. For most companies, this vision sounds like the impossible dream. Each of these groups has their own distinctive personality, culture, language, and view on human capital.

Asking HR and procurement to work together may seem like trying to mix oil and water. For starters, they don't even speak the same human capital language. HR uses terms such as talent, recruiting, compensation, and benefits. Whereas, procurement uses terms such as services procurement, labor-based categories, labor-related spend, spend under management, and cost containment. The two completely different languages reflect their very different views on human capital.

HR and procurement often work as if their goals are mutually exclusive. But manufacturing supply chain management results have shown us that quality can be improved while costs are reduced.

HR and procurement may believe they understand each other, but there has not been a deep enough understanding of each other's strengths and weaknesses to truly integrate their efforts and benefit from the synergy. The CEO must require that the organization move beyond silos and become a true team, whose members bring their strengths to the table and work together, learn to speak a shared language, and transform the supply chain.

DEFINE YOUR STRATEGIC TALENT MIX

In the U.S., there has been a longstanding bias toward hiring a permanent and direct workforce. There are so many more types of employment that must now be considered, including: part-time, temporary, contractor, consultants, and outsourced workers. In a complex and competitive environment, corporations must decide which type of talent is the best fit in each situation, and that's not so simple. Companies need a strategic workforce plan, a methodology for making talent-mix decisions along with supporting processes and integrated technologies. Building a just-in-time human capital supply chain is a big commitment, but has the potential for big returns.

SET HCSC GOALS

The staffing and recruitment industries have been working on key metrics through several organizations, but no shortlist of key metrics has yet been widely accepted or adopted. There is an enormous need to follow manufacturing's example and define a holistic set of HCSC measurements and embed them directly into the technology that automates the HCSCM process.

HR organizations have been slow to jump on the key performance indicator (KPI) and scorecard bandwagon. Most staffing agencies, on the other hand, are much more numbers-driven. Because staffing has their own profit centers, they tend to be much more engaged by the performance data, even down to the individual recruiter level. They also tend to understand the interrelationships between metrics that cross their organization, e.g. recruiters routinely calculate the profitability of each placement.

HR organizations are increasingly aware that they must optimize their process efficiency and performance; but they tend to think of themselves as a "cost" center rather than a "profit" center, plagued by never-ending cost reduction programs. The availability of up-to-date performance data in other areas of their organization pressures HR to accelerate their metrics definition and performance improvement processes. Clearly, there are a lot of lessons learned from manufacturing SCM that can be applied effectively to benefit the HCSC.

ENGAGE YOUR STRATEGIC SUPPLIERS

Before supply chain management philosophies took hold, suppliers were treated as vendors who needed to be pressured and coerced into performing. SCM gurus understood that having a few key suppliers could become a strategic advantage if they were helped by their clients to be more successful. Tightening the relationship with a handful of capable suppliers meant vendors "opened the kimono" and shared proprietary processes, planning data, and even problems. In many cases, software was integrated between companies so that planning, production, and inventory data could be shared in real time. Manufacturers blurred the line with their suppliers in an effort to eliminate hand-off issues and accelerate production. Having more reliable intelligence about production meant that suppliers could partner to take cost out of the supply chain and reflect that in preferred pricing.

Staffing suppliers, as well as buyers, often see themselves as a commodity and there is nothing strategic in a commodity purchase. Some HR and procurement buyers recognize their dependence on staffing suppliers and work to develop longer-term relationships, yet average staffing contracts are in the three-year range, nowhere near the ten-year commitment that manufacturing firms make for their gains.

Cheaper prices can be offered and great profits earned when costs are taken out anywhere and everywhere across the supply chain. SCM managers learned that it took the whole supply chain, working in concert and focused on the same goals to achieve these lofty and attractive rewards.

No Excuses, Get Started

In a knowledge economy, people are the engine that makes the company "go." The total cost of human capital is a massive expense. Understanding the cost is essential so that action can be taken to make the HCSC more effective and efficient. Even small improvements in the HCSC (e.g. small rate changes) have a ripple effect that can add up to meaningful cost savings. By putting a HCSC management program in place, it becomes possible to continue to find ways to better manage cost while increasing the quality of the workforce. We must manage our human capital as efficiently and effectively as we manage all of the other parts of our business.

Translating manufacturing supply chain lessons learned to the HCSC is an obvious idea and makes perfect business sense. Companies often hesitate to get started because so many entrenched roles must change, and the ideas, as applied to human capital, feel so unfamiliar. Companies new to HCSC programs can kick off their program in a number of tenable ways, including consolidating and tiering vendors, implementing a vendor management system, conducting a human capital spend analysis, writing a strategic workforce plan, or documenting and analyzing the current HCSC process.

HR professionals need to be more scientific about how they size, plan, and shape their workforce. Procurement needs to shift more attention to understanding and managing human capital spend. Corporations must develop strategic supplier relationships in order to hire the best-fit talent. Executives need to stop viewing human capital as an HR issue and become more engaged in strategizing and planning their workforce, since their workforce is most likely their most mission-critical asset and their greatest financial expense. Management can leverage the same diligence and discipline in managing their HCSC that they apply to the rest of their business.

Chapter 2: Thirty Years of Manufacturing Supply Chain Experience

CHAPTER OBJECTIVES:

- Explain key manufacturing supply chain management concepts so that they can be easily applied to the HCSC in later chapters.

- Identify and appreciate the unique characteristics of the human capital supply chain.

LEARNING FROM THIRTY YEARS OF MANUFACTURING SUPPLY CHAIN MANAGEMENT

A Brief History Lesson

"The term 'supply chain management' arose in the late 1980s and came into widespread use in the 1990s."[1] Supply chains encompass the companies that create the end product or service and all of their suppliers and sub-suppliers. "Supply chain management covers all of the business activities needed to design, make, deliver, and use a product or service."[2] In *The 7 Principles of Supply Chain Management*, the authors Anderson, Britt, and Favre define supply chain management more broadly: "We can define supply chain management as the things we do to influence the behavior of the supply chain and get the results we want."[3]

"Businesses depend on their supply chains to provide them with what they need to survive and thrive"[4] and supply chain management breakdowns can make headline news and kill financial results. Companies have spent decades improving their supply chain processes and technologies because the results have meant lower operating costs, higher quality products, higher levels of customer satisfaction, and the opportunity for greater revenues and profits.

Supply Chain Management Frameworks

The Supply-Chain Council introduced the Supply Chain Operations Reference-model (SCOR) in 1996 to help manufacturing companies measure process improvements across supply chain organizations. The Supply-Chain Council's fifty or so participating organizations (e.g. AT&T Wireless, Boeing, Coca-Cola, and Unilever) jointly developed the widely adopted SCOR model.

The SCOR model includes five key supply chain management processes: Plan, Source, Make, Deliver, and Return. The model focuses on driving several key performance attributes for supply chains, namely: reliability, flexibility, responsiveness, cost, and asset management. The SCOR model has been updated regularly and now supports a wider set of industries (e.g. retail, service providers) and trends (e.g. e-business, environmental sustainability).

1. **Plan**. This is the strategic portion of supply chain management wherein companies conduct demand and supply planning for their end product or service. A big piece of SCM planning is developing a set of metrics to monitor the supply chain so that it is efficient, costs less, and delivers high-quality products and value to customers.

2. **Source.** Companies choose preferred suppliers to deliver the goods and services that they need to create their end products. Supply chain managers develop a set of pricing, delivery, and payment processes with suppliers, and create metrics for managing supplier performance. Sourcing also includes inventory management, just-in-time receiving, and electronic supplier payment authorization.

3. **Make.** Supply chain managers schedule and manage production, testing, packaging, and delivery preparation. This is the most metric-intensive portion of the supply chain — wherein companies are able to measure quality levels, production output, worker productivity, and production costs.[5]

4. **Deliver.** Many SCM insiders refer to this part as logistics, wherein companies coordinate the just-in-time receipt of orders from customers, manage a network of warehouses, pick carriers to take products to customers and set up an invoicing system to receive payments.[6]

5. **Return.** Because return is often a problematic part of the supply chain for companies, supply chain planners have to create a responsive and flexible network for receiving back defective and excess products from their customers (i.e. reverse logistics management). SCOR's return process category also includes the customer service and support function.

The SCOR model is widely adopted and well respected, but it is not the only supply chain management framework. The American Productivity and Quality Center (APQC) supports cross-company and cross-industry benchmarking of supply chain planning, procurement, manufacturing, and logistics. Based on the efforts of eighty participating organizations, APQC has identified the crucial set of supply chain performance indicators that are needed to accurately measure performance and capture performance data on a worldwide basis.

Supply chain management methodologies and technologies continue to evolve. What had been narrowly defined as logistics, procurement, distribution, maintenance, and inventory management, now also includes marketing, new product development, finance, and customer service. Further, the types of companies leveraging supply chain management principles continue to expand. *Industry Week's* David Blanchard noted in 2008 that leading supply chains include traditional physical manufacturing and assembly companies (e.g. Toyota), entertainment companies (e.g. Disney), and electronic products (e.g. iTunes).[7]

SEVEN GREAT SCM CONCEPTS AND LESSONS LEARNED

Much can be said to repackage manufacturing supply chain concepts for HCSC practitioners. But we will focus on a handful of key concepts that have been developed and refined over the last several decades. These valuable tools can be easily applied to the HCSC to gain the very same industry-saving benefits achieved by the manufacturing industry — lower operational costs and increased quality.

Build quality into the process through continuous improvement.

One of the key and fundamental steps in any supply chain management program is that all business processes must be documented. The International Organization for Standardization offers the ISO 9000 set of standards, which provides a way to document and manage key processes. In our experience, few HCSC management processes are actually documented. There appears to be a great deal of resistance to documentation and the standardization of processes across corporations. However, there is no way to dramatically improve any process without documentation and performance metrics.

Six Sigma and Total Quality Management (TQM) are philosophies and methodologies adopted by many SCM programs to facilitate supply chain improvements. These approaches teach management to continually remove product defects by systematically identifying and addressing inefficiencies and customer service issues. The problem causing the greatest negative impact is addressed first, but all issues are addressed over time. Tools such as the Pareto chart, a bar graph that shows the relative frequency of each issue, is used by management to focus on the problems that are causing the greatest number of defects first. The idea being: focusing on the most important twenty percent of the problem will fix eighty percent of the defects (the 80/20 Rule).

In some cases, major infrastructure changes are required to fix the number-one issue. In these situations, problems that are easier to fix but have less impact on the organization ("low-hanging fruit") may be addressed first. Once the main problems to be addressed are identified, root cause analysis techniques are applied to uncover all of the contributing factors. The problems are then grouped and linked until the root causes of the problem are identified. Fishbone diagrams (cause-and-effect diagrams, also known as Ishikawa after the inventor) provide a useful way of displaying the related causes of key problems.

Root causes are addressed based on their impact, with the most impactful issues resolved first. Once fixes are implemented, they are measured and any necessary adjustments are made to maximize improvements. A systematic Plan-Do-Check-Act feedback loop is put into place so that once the root cause is understood and a solution put in place, the performance is continually measured and tuned.

Supply chains are not perfected overnight and usually require several years to fully implement. Rather, improvement is achieved through disciplined and continuous analysis of issues and elimination of defects. Defects, especially those that result in returns, scrap, or rework are expensive to the organization, and catching defective parts and products before they reach the customer saves everyone money. While defects may be minimized, continuous process and quality improvement programs are never-ending; improvements are always possible.

Achieving the best match between a worker and a job is so much harder than achieving zero defects in manufacturing because there are so many unique aspects to the fit. Where production lines focus on parts, assembly, machinery, and the like, successful staffing means that the person not only has the appropriate skills, but they fit into the team and the surrounding company culture. Overqualified workers can create as much or more productivity issues, and of course worker performance can change over time depending on personal factors such as how they feel about the work, their health, and whatever else is going on in their lives. Hiring managers need to be able to accurately assess candidate quality before accepting the candidate. Minimizing defects in the HCSC adds many more dimensions of complexity when compared to the manufacturing case, but documenting and continuously improving the HCSC process in order to match the best worker to the work and optimize worker performance is clearly a worthy goal.

Enable just in time (JIT) inventory across the entire supply chain.

Elimination of unnecessary inventory has always been a key concept of the traditional manufacturing supply chain. "The primary purpose of inventory is to act as a buffer against uncertainty in the supply chain. However, holding inventory can be expensive" [8] and companies who know their optimal inventory levels are able to keep their costs low. Component parts and finished products sitting in warehouses entail storage fees. An additional risk is that the product will not be sold or the component parts will become obsolete before they are sold, creating unnecessary waste. The ideal situation is when the exact set of component parts arrives for assembly with enough time to create the product so that it can be distributed to the consumer at the exact moment they wish to make their purchase. The same just-in-time concept can prove to be highly effective when applied to people inventory in a HCSC environment.

JIT world-class manufacturing means the right product is produced and delivered to the consumer at the right time and at the right cost and for the right price. JIT human capital means that the right talent is located and delivered to the worksite at the right time and for the right cost. The human capital provided must have the correct attributes required to complete the work effort. That means the right combination of education, skills, experience, and personality.

Minimal waste and JIT delivery is required at every step along either supply chain. In order to achieve this objective, companies need to measure, manage, and account for lead times at each hand-off. Great planning, process knowledge, real-time data, and continuous communication between all parties is required, otherwise expensive rush orders for components (or people) result.

Idle production-line capacity is as problematic as excess inventory, because it also represents unnecessary cost such as scrap and rework that is attached to the final product. From a talent perspective, this equates to a surplus of skills or the underutilization of existing resources. Just as manufacturers operate their manufacturing lines at capacity, organizations aim for a highly utilized, highly productive workforce.

The manufacturing industry took a long time to get behind JIT inventory as a worthy and achievable goal, but the resulting cost savings and competitive advantage motivated industry-wide adoption.

There is a lot of resistance and discomfort involved in equating people with inventory, and JIT talent sounds like an unachievable goal. First of all, leveraging JIT concepts does not mean equating people to components. Rather, this is an effort to make more of a science out of workforce planning, integrated technologies, and resource management. During the mass layoffs of the 2009 recession, it became obvious that a fine-tuned method for identifying excess in the HCSC was greatly needed.

Build a metrics-driven performance-oriented organization.

As the manufacturing supply chain experts learned in the 1980s, "If you don't measure it, you can't manage it." Whatever the approach — control charts, quad graphs, key performance indicators, or balanced scorecards — supply chain management focused on specific and measurable goals. Process changes were no longer based on management instinct or experience. Rather, analysis and study suggested the root cause of problems. Once management put process changes in place, the resulting improvements could be tracked against the expected outcome to validate and prove a positive impact. Manufacturing supply chain management developed a highly disciplined and objective method for process performance management.

A variety of measures were identified and painstakingly defined by supply chain experts and management teams. While cycle times, quality tests, and cost measures were identified on a process-by-process basis, end-to-end measures were even more important since handoffs between processes were found to be at particular risk for poor communication and unintended consequences. Further, customer-focused metrics were carefully articulated and all inwardly facing metrics were tied together, creating a metrics hierarchy. A great deal of new customer satisfaction measurements and methodology were birthed during the '80s and '90s.

HR has never had a numbers-driven culture like the early days of manufacturing. Workforce management decisions are often made based on experience, gut feel, intuition, and other subjective criteria. While there will always be an art to managing people, there is clearly also room for more science.

The staffing and recruitment industries have been working on key metrics through several organizations, including the Society of Human Resources Management (SHRM), International Association for Human Resources Information (IHRIM), Staffing.org, American Staffing Association (ASA), and Staffing Industry Analysts (SIA), but no shortlist of key metrics has yet been widely accepted and adopted. There is an enormous need to follow manufacturing's example and define a holistic set of HCSC measures and embed them directly into the technology that automates the HCSCM process.

HR organizations have been slow to jump on the KPI and scorecard bandwagon. Many staffing agencies, on the other hand, are much more numbers-driven. Because staffing has their own profit center, they tend to be much more engaged by the performance data, even down to the individual recruiter level, and they tend to understand the interrelationships between metrics that cross their organization, e.g. recruiters routinely calculate the profitability of each placement. HR organizations are increasingly aware that they must optimize their process efficiency and performance. The availability of up-to-date performance data in other areas of their organization pressures HR to accelerate their metrics definition and performance improvement processes. Clearly, there are a lot of lessons learned from manufacturing SCM that can be effectively applied to benefit the HCSC.

Value strategic supplier relationships, and treat the supply chain as a single entity.

In the 1990s, manufacturing realized that their success was dependent on their supplier's success. Before supply chain management philosophies took hold, suppliers were treated as vendors who needed to be pressured and coerced into performing. SCM gurus understood that a few key, strategic suppliers could create strategic advantage. Tightening the relationship with a handful of capable suppliers meant vendors "opened the kimono" and shared proprietary processes, planning data, and even problems. In many cases, software was integrated between companies so that planning, production, and inventory data could be shared in real time. Manufacturers blurred the line with their suppliers in an effort to eliminate hand-off issues and speed production. Having greater commitment from their buyers and having more reliable intelligence about production meant that suppliers could truly partner to remove cost from the entire supply chain and reflect that with preferred pricing.

Staffing suppliers as well as buyers often see themselves as a commodity, and there is nothing strategic in a commodity purchase. Some HR and procurement buyers recognize their dependence on staffing suppliers and work to develop longer-term relationships; yet average staffing contracts are in the three-year range, nowhere near the ten-year commitment that manufacturing firms make for their gains.

Cheaper prices can be offered and great profits earned when costs are taken out anywhere and everywhere across the entire supply chain. Manufacturing supply chain managers learned that it took the whole supply chain, working in concert and focused on the same goals, to achieve these lofty and attractive goals.

Eliminate waste and duplicate effort.

In his 1988 book, *Toyota Production System*, Taiichi Ohno outlined the seven most-common manufacturing wastes: overproduction, inventory, waiting, transportation (e.g. unnecessary handling), non-value-added motion, non-value-added processing or over-processing, and defects. In 1990 James Womack, coined the term "lean" manufacturing in his book, *The Machine that Changed the World* and the concept of eliminating waste expanded into an entire lean enterprise movement over the next twenty years. Lean thought leaders, such as Womack, started to extend lean thinking to include another form of waste, the underutilization of workers.

There is much waste and duplication of effort across the human capital supply chain. A simple example is when a job requisition is distributed to multiple suppliers who then all post the same job on the same job boards. Even though the hiring company only pays one staffing firm for that placement, the operating costs for all the staffing firms that attempted to fill the position increases, which is eventually passed on in future placements. A more extreme example is when hiring companies who conduct their own recruitment and also use staffing suppliers have duplicate recruiting teams, processes, technology, and costs. There is a great deal of work to be done in order to eliminate duplicate efforts and minimize HCSC costs.

Systematically take cost out while increasing quality.

According *to The Essentials of Supply Chain Management*, "Effective supply chain management requires simultaneous improvement in both customer service levels and the internal operating efficiencies of all companies in the supply chain. Customer service at its most basic level means consistently high order fill rates, high on-time delivery rates, and a very low rate of products returned by customers for whatever reason. Internal efficiency for organizations in a supply chain means that these organizations get an attractive rate of return on their investments in inventory and find ways to lower their operating and sales expenses."[9]

Product quality is much easier to measure than the quality of human capital, especially when quality needs to be assessed before the person is on the job. Hiring managers and staffing suppliers would love to be able to accurately assess the quality of talent in the hiring process. Personality, behavioral, and skills assessments are more frequently included as required quality screening steps. Staffing suppliers often promise they will provide higher quality talent than their competition, but the claim is difficult to prove. HCSC stakeholders must find a way to measure and assess the quality of talent as early in the talent acquisition process as possible. While it seems impossible, HCSCs must follow the manufacturing example and deliver higher quality results while lowering costs.

Get CEO-level buy-in.

Management of the supply chain requires coordination between diverse departments across the organization. Finance, procurement, and production must all work together to hone the manufacturing supply chain. In manufacturing, C-level directives and focus are required before true collaboration and change can take place.

The importance of CEO buy-in and ongoing involvement is absolutely essential to any successful HCSC implementation. It is the strategic responsibility of every CEO to grasp the connection between strategic growth and the streamlining of the HCSC through the use of improved processes and technology. According to Booz, Allen, and Hamilton thought leaders, "A top-down SCM approach that is, an initiative endorsed and led by the chief executive officer — is critical to securing senior management buy-in and ensuring that the strategy will yield good results. A Booz Allen Hamilton survey found that companies that assign SCM to functional leaders achieve fifty-five percent less in savings than those where the CEO plays a hands-on role in linking SCM to overall corporate strategy.[10]

SIMILARITIES AND DIFFERENCES

Manufacturing supply chain concepts, frameworks, and tools remained well developed after thirty years thanks to the collaboration of hundreds of corporations around the globe. Procurement professionals have started to apply their manufacturing supply chain expertise to the HCSC, but the differences between the manufacturing supply chain and the HCSC are meaningful and require additional skills, processes, and tools. While many concepts and methods translate well from manufacturing to human capital, there are fundamental differences between managing a supply chain that procures goods and a supply chain that hires people.

Goods are uniform and people are unique. There are as many product stock keeping units (SKUs) as there are people. While there may be standardized job titles, skill names, competencies, pay ranges, etc., within the organization, there is nothing exactly like a product parts list for people. Each worker is a unique combination of a complex set of attributes including skills, experience, and personality.

Matching candidates to a job opening often requires the good judgment of recruiters and an understanding of the complex trade-offs hiring managers are willing to make. The match between worker and work not only considers what the worker offers, but also factors in the worker's desire for the specific position. Goods have no preferences or career plans that need to be considered. Clearly, sourcing people is more complex than sourcing goods.

People negotiate their own availability, price, and terms. Each and every placement requires negotiation around availability, pay, and employment terms. The worker generally conducts these negotiations for themselves. When staffing suppliers are used, bill rates are negotiated with the hiring company. Volume pricing and standardized pricing may apply, but the staffing supplier must negotiate the pay rate with each worker individually. Goods certainly do not have a say in setting their own prices and terms.

Goods are received once; services are received on an ongoing basis. Service billings and reporting are much more complex for people than for goods. For example, a component is purchased by an enterprise at a specific price, to arrive at a specific time, at which the purchase order will reflect receipt of the component and zero the balance due for that item. For human capital procurement, purchase orders are based on estimates; they typically overrun, involve change requests for extensions, and run down at a variable rate.

People perform inconsistently. It is impossible for people to perform consistently and maintain steady productivity levels. Minute by minute, day to day, year to year worker performance will vary because humans are emotional beings with many factors at play. While product and equipment performance may deteriorate over time, the breakdown is gradual and predictable. Over- and under-utilization are difficult to measure and tune and, at the same time, workers are sensitive to their level of boredom, burnout, and engagement.

The value of people to the corporation increases with their length of service. Once people are hired their skills and experience continue to evolve, their value to the consuming organization continually changes. By working at a company for a certain amount of time, workers gain an organizational awareness that adds value. They may also gain new skills through coaching, training, or just experience on the job. Alternatively, if you don't use a skill, it becomes "stale." Goods don't increase their value to the corporation over time, in fact, their decreasing value or depreciation is scheduled.

People can walk away; products can't. Employers can terminate employment in the U.S. with very little effort or obligation ("at will"). Non-contract employees may terminate employment at any time and may even stop showing up to work without any penalty. Companies invest in their human capital through coaching, training, managing, developing, and career planning. But at the end of the day, the employee can walk out the door on any given day, taking that investment and skill set with them.

While the physical aspects of manufacturing create a number of notable differences, the fundamental components of the human capital and manufacturing supply chains are quite similar. The decades of study and lessons learned that can be applied to the HCSC are far too valuable to dismiss.

KEY POINTS: LESSONS FROM MANUFACTURING

- Money usually flows one way in the HCSC. Corporations need to step up their efforts and optimize their supply chains. Staffing suppliers need to understand how their role is enabling their clients' success.

- A tremendous amount of money can be saved by corporations who apply manufacturing SCM practices to the HCSC.

- Systematically and continuously remove costs from the supply chain by eliminating inefficiencies.

- Make a science out of matching workers with work tasks and keeping them optimally utilized.

- Resist making excuses and proactively invest in business process documentation and KPIs, in order to truly track, measure, and manage the HCSC.

- Orient the organization around key metrics and continuously improve the supply chain by acting on performance data that is monitored weekly and eventually daily.

- An organization-specific, strategic workforce plan is essential to drive a firm's HCSC.

- Hire experienced, data-driven workforce planners to develop the strategic workforce plan.

- Invest in long-term supplier relationships to get the lowest cost and highest quality staffing organization.

- CEO buy-in is a critical success factor, and any HCSCM program will be tough to launch without the CEO on board.

Chapter 3: Craft the Business Case for HCSCM

Chapter objectives:

- Explain the many benefits of the HCSC.
- Sketch the high-level ROI to validate the feasibility of an HCSCM program.
- Provide sample HCSC KPIs to track progress and demonstrate ROI.

Estimate Return-on-Investment for Your Human Capital Supply Chain Management (HCSCM) Program

Investments must be made in the HCSC before it is possible to reap the massive benefits, such as spend visibility, cost savings, higher-quality talent, and increased revenues. Implementing an HCSC is a major business transformation effort that requires a multi-stage, multi-year program. Once the HCSC strategy and plan are developed, a set of process, technology, organizational and change management projects can be identified. Each project must be justified with a comprehensive cost/benefit analysis. Rapid return on investment is expected for each project or small group of projects. Further investment in the program is contingent on proven success at frequent milestones along the way.

In order to make the decision to develop a HCSCM strategy and implementation plan, executives must be confident that establishing a HCSC will yield substantial ROI and long-lasting benefits. The business case depends on a high-level analysis of the firm's current company-wide human capital and an understanding of the costs and benefits that will be achieved with the implementation and ongoing management of the HCSC.

The way to begin is by outlining a conceptual business case, which is a qualitative explanation of the ROI. From there, work on identifying the metrics that best align with the conceptual business case and business goals. These metrics might also be called the key performance indicators. Once these are identified and defined the measurement of current performance serves as a baseline. Using industry associations or peer groups, benchmarking data must be gathered in order to set realistic improvement goals. The next step is to develop solution and project plans that describe the steps to be taken to enable the HCSC change. After estimating the costs associated with the planned solutions and projects, it is time to calculate ROI. Because HCSCM is a continuous improvement effort, it is necessary to identify ways to change the HCSC to generate additional ROI.

High-Level Benefits of a HCSCM Program

Spend visibility. Very little gain can be made in the area of HCSCM without having full and continuous visibility into company-wide human capital spend related to employees, temps, contractors, consultants, business service providers, and outsourcers. Measuring human capital spend is a mandatory first step to any HCSCM program and needs to be driven by the CFO and the procurement team. Transparent spend means that senior managers have spending data on which they can take action to streamline their human capital processes. With greater ability to take control over their operation, management can drive up human capital performance and drive down related costs. Visibility shines the spotlight on sweetheart deals with talent suppliers and creates organizational pressure to bring maverick spend in line with consistent market rates.

Cost savings through greater process efficiency. Vendor management system (VMS) case studies show five to twenty percent costs savings to the hiring company in the first year a VMS program is implemented. Much of this cost savings is attributed to the consolidation, tiering, and more consistent management of suppliers, and the leveling of bill rates. VMS implementation includes a review of all suppliers, their rates, and the inconsistent processes that usually exist between similar vendors. Rates are typically audited by procurement and analyzed for consistency between divisions and hiring managers within the same company. Rates are adjusted downward as volume and longer-term commitments can be achieved and consolidated across the company. Further cost savings are realized as subsequent worker types, business units, skill types, and geographies are included in the program. Each portion of the rollout will yield varying levels of return, depending on a number of factors. For example, making even a small change in the bill rate for a skill set that is procured in volume will yield more than a larger change in rate for a low-paid, low-volume skill set.

Cost savings associated with VMS are impressive. Because HCSCM is a relatively new concept, VMS provides a great example of the potential cost savings that are possible.

Automation across HCSC processes greatly reduces manual work and increases the consistency of business processes and practices. Non-standard processes are less efficient for companies and are more expensive to manage.

The integration of consistent processes and systems also reduces duplicate data entry and speeds communication between all parties. Integrating the technology that automates the HCSC speeds the movement of job orders and candidates through the entire supply chain so that talent needs can be filled as quickly as possible with the best candidate starting on the desired start date.

As with the VMS example, job orders and candidates need to be entered into each entity's systems in the supply chain. When external agencies are used to fill positions, the job order and candidates must be entered manually into the corporate ATS, the VMS, and the staffing supplier's front office system. Integrating systems means that the data is exchanged automatically and on a real-time basis, reducing duplicate data entry across the supply chain, reducing data entry errors, and speeding communication.

The HCSC strategy results in an optimal talent mix — the mix of worker types that delivers the best value to the company. Calculating and managing to the optimal talent mix will reduce the overall cost of labor to the corporation.

Staffing levels and rates are typically adjusted annually or as needed. Increasing the frequency of staffing level reviews to monthly or even weekly will ensure that current staffing levels and market-level bill rates will drive optimal productivity and minimize underutilization or overutilization of key talent. Contract and rate compliance must be tightly monitored and audited, to ensure that hiring companies are paying the agreed-upon rates. Further, rates can be adjusted more often to reflect even the smallest fluctuations in the market.

Elimination of waste and duplicated work efforts will all drive cost out of the supply chain. One small example of waste is the number of times the same job posting is placed on the same job boards by competing suppliers who are trying to fill the same exact job order. HCSC best practices will greatly reduce this and all kinds of duplication.

As we have seen with the manufacturing supply chain, continuous improvement of the supply chain processes never stops. Process improvement programs require continuous analysis of the current situation to identify opportunities to drive out cost and improve quality.

Higher quality of talent. Efficient HCSCs ensure faster access to better talent. By speeding time-to-fill and honing talent acquisition processes, hiring companies can be sure to identify qualified and available talent faster than the competition.

Corporations usually spend considerable time and money trying to streamline their external hiring practices but, unfortunately, they do not spend an equal amount of effort developing internal mobility processes. It is not uncommon for a hiring manager to request an external candidate because they do not have access to the updated skills and preferences of their existing employee base. You may also know of instances where a manager selfishly blocks current employees from new internal job opportunities in order to keep a good employee from leaving. An integrated HCSC eliminates these problems by giving existing employees first access to new internal opportunities electronically.

Shared definitions of skills and competencies across the supply chain provide another method for streamlining the process and can ensure that candidates clearly meet the job requirements. When all parties in the supply chain use the same language to describe the job and the candidates, better matches are made.

Increased revenue. Well-managed HCSCs mean that all positions are filled just in time, with the highest quality talent who can start on the desired date. This is a critical goal for any HCSC and this goal must permeate throughout all plans and communications. Because there are fewer unfilled positions in the highly efficient HCSC world, revenues increase.

Individuals responsible for implementing and running a HCSC will initially feel that achieving just-in-time, high-quality talent on the desired start date is an impossible task. In our manufacturing analogy, it was initially impossible for everyone to imagine a 99.99 percent quality level, until it was actually achieved within the factory.

Strategic competitive advantage. The combination of decreased costs, higher-quality talent and increased revenues means that those firms who implement an efficient HCSC are at a strategic competitive advantage. As firms around the world begin to come out of the global recession, the need for a more streamlined and automated HCSC is evident.

As we learned in manufacturing, establishing and managing a supply chain not only reduces costs in the short term, but the long-term tuning of the supply chain can result in unprecedented growth and strategic competitive advantage.

High-Level Costs of a HCSCM Program

Each portion of the HCSC implementation is likely to have costs associated with business process design and implementation, technology, training, and change management.

Investments around the automation of the HCSC are the greatest expense. As the current set of applications is reviewed, and the required assessment of the new technologies is done to identify the system integrations points, the resulting cost of technology is likely to be quite high. While expected technology expense may seem enormous, it will be dwarfed by the cost savings that will occur by implementing the HCSCM program. Ideally the HCSCM implementation program is designed to generate cost savings through process and policy changes so that the savings freed up can be utilized to fund technology initiatives.

Take cost out; don't just push cost down the chain.

The vendor management system market demonstrates the importance of considering costs across the entire supply chain. A VMS follows a supplier-funded model, meaning that staffing suppliers pay a percentage of their revenues to the VMS provider, typically one to three percent. Implementing a VMS requires the hiring company to pay little or no capital toward getting VMS programs off the ground. Low or no start-up costs mean that the VMS takes money "off the top" for the life of the program. Even though it may look like VMS costs are passed to the supplier, savvy hiring companies understand that they are still funding the VMS, just via the suppliers. When calculating HSCS costs, it is important to ensure that costs are not just moving from one part of the supply chain to another.

Getting the conceptual business case approved

A conceptual business case will be a high-level, quantitative analysis of the overall costs and benefits of the HCSCM program. Before investing too much time or effort in new ideas, most companies first justify new strategic initiatives at a conceptual level. The conceptual HCSCM business case will inspire key stakeholders to support the idea, articulate the persuasive business rationale for moving forward with the HCSCM program, and estimate the size of the financial opportunity.

HCSCM projects can be quite difficult to get approved in spite of their fast and impressive ROI. As we've seen with VMS, the approval process to move forward with the program can stall, even with virtually guaranteed ROI. As in the VMS case, we can expect the approval of a HCSCM initiative to be tricky because project costs and benefits span multiple departments, making it difficult for a single business unit to move forward.

Approval for a conceptual HCSCM business case will come more quickly when the project sponsor is a C-level executive and is able to consider the value of the project from the overall business's point of view. Without C-level ownership of the HCSCM program, the organization will not be able to maintain the long-term, enterprise-wide support necessary for the success of the program.

KPIs, Benchmarks, and Performance Management

Metrics and benchmarks can be used to develop additional qualitative details to support the ROI in a conceptual HCSCM business case, but they must be used to calculate the ROI for specific HCSCM projects.

Once key performance indicators are selected, current performance is baselined, and benchmark data is gathered. It is then possible to estimate the achievable and measurable improvements that the HCSCM projects will provide.

Sources of Metrics and Benchmarking Data

A number of industry organizations have attempted to identify, define, and benchmark key HR metrics. While much work has been done in this area, there is no single set of metrics to use; so, it is necessary to consider the options and decide which metrics and KPIs will be most pertinent to the specific HCSC.

Without a true industry standard, companies will need to investigate the sources of metrics and benchmarking data and decide where they want to start.

Society of Human Resource Management (SHRM). SHRM offers both metrics and benchmarking. Their HR Metrics Toolkit provides downloadable spreadsheet templates to calculate and compile HR metrics and various types of HR and other business reports. After entering key data, the sample templates use embedded formulas to calculate key data like cost per hire, time to fill, health cost per employee, and human capital ROI. SHRM's benchmarking database includes more than 140 metrics and data from over five-thousand organizations. Data can be pulled by industry and workforce size. The HR Metrics Toolkit and other publications about HR metrics are free for SHRM members. But SHRM charges a fee for benchmarking reports and customized benchmarking services.

Saratoga Institute. The Saratoga Institute, owned by PricewaterhouseCoopers (PwC), provides human capital measurement and benchmarking data and consulting services. Saratoga's HR Index™ is a benchmarking database that contains more than three hundred people-performance metrics from at least 10,500 international organizations. Saratoga's metrics cover organization and operations, HR staff and structure, compensation and benefits, hiring and staffing, and retention and separations. Saratoga also offers an annual country-specific Human Capital Effectiveness Survey Report. The U.S. version contains results from more than three-hundred organizations.

Staffing.org. Staffing.org offers annual metrics research for the staffing and recruiting functions within HR. The Staffing.org Recruiting Metrics and Benchmark Report is a good source for annual updates of key industry recruiting metrics. The Job Seekers and Employees Report analyzes Internet behavior of job seekers by education, age, ethnicity, job title, salary level, geography, and gender. The report includes metrics, trended data, and best practices for time and cost metrics, hiring manager satisfaction, candidate quality, and retention.

Open Standards Benchmarking Collaborative (OSBC). The American Productivity and Quality Center (APQC) conducts human capital management benchmarking surveys as part of their larger Open Standards Benchmarking Collaborative (OSBC) initiative. More than 1,800 companies are involved in the benchmarking surveys, which cover HR organization, HR policies and strategy, recruitment, training and development, reward and retention, payroll, and more. OSBC benchmarking is open to all organizations globally as APQC purposely defines the metrics in such a way that they are applicable internationally. Participants receive a detailed report that compares their response to median and top performers in their industry. The research is underwritten by IBM and available at no cost to survey participants.

Staffing Industry Benchmarking Consortium (SIBC). The SIBC, managed by Staffing Industry Analysts (SIA), consists of a wide-variety of staffing companies who confidentially provide financial and operating data on a quarterly basis. Sales data, including margins, and operating and infrastructure expenses are captured. Participating staffing firms can access aggregated reports and survey results, segmented by staffing specialty and size, free of charge.

American Staffing Association (ASA). ASA is a good source for staffing firm metrics and benchmarks. ASA has been conducting an Operations Survey on temporary and contract staffing as well as placement and recruiting services since 1998. The ASA Operations Survey collects information for the prior fiscal year on staffing company sales, expenses, profits, and personnel performance metrics. The final survey report is segmented by business size and staffing sector. Both members and non-members may purchase the Operations Survey Report.

The ASA has also developed a Staffing Index that provides a national measure of staffing industry employment and estimates weekly changes in the number of temporary and contract workers. The Staffing Index is based on data obtained through a secure web-based questionnaire completed by staffing firms. Participants receive a weekly email report on the survey results and the data is also available on ASA's website.

Additional sources. Other sources of HR and staffing metrics and benchmarking data include: The Bureau of Labor Statistics (BLS), The Bureau of National Affairs (BNA), The Institute of Management and Administration, Inc (IOMA), the Employers Association Development Group (EADG), the International Public Management Association for Human Resources (IPMA-HR), the HR Metrics Center, the Association of Executive Search Consultants (AESC) and the TechServe Alliance (formerly NACCB). We also expect that Software as a Service (SaaS) based technology (e.g. VMS) will present the opportunity for software vendors to provide benchmarking data.

Sample Key Metrics

Metrics must include both quantitative and qualitative performance measures — end-to-end and process-specific metrics. Corporations also need to measure process hand-offs, which may require including metrics in service level agreements (SLAs) with strategic suppliers.

There are several hundred HR metrics. Each organization defines metrics uniquely so it is up to each individual organization to research the options. Some examples of the metrics that are most important to HR organizations (with our HCSC theme):

- Actual to planned human capital spend;
- Percentage human capital spend savings;
- Percentage human capital utilization;
- Revenue per human capital resource;
- Percentage of positions filled;
- Time to hire, including time to screen, time to submit, time to interview, and time to offer;
- Time to productivity;
- Cost per hire;
- Vacancy rate and cost of vacancy;
- Actual to expected human capital performance;
- Turnover, turnover rate, and cost of turnover;
- Satisfaction levels, including hiring manager, candidate, and supplier;
- Payroll metrics (e.g. number of payroll errors, number of checks, and cost per payroll payment).
- Staffing firms also need to add billing and payment measures.

Performance Management

Routine analysis of performance data and continuous improvement methods ensures that the ROI expected from the HCSCM projects is achieved.

Leverage dashboards for performance visibility. As we learned with the manufacturing supply chain, each and every worker needs to be engaged with the program goals in order to maximize performance. Summary reports used to typically be one-page reports tacked on a bulletin board, but dashboards are more often projected on LCD screens in work areas or incorporated into core software applications. Dashboards provide a set of summary metrics, which assess the health of the worker's area of responsibility. Much like the dashboard in a car, the worker's dashboard is visually appealing and includes charts, graphs, and visual clues about status and current performance levels. Dashboards tell workers if they are on course relative to expected performance levels. Further analysis of performance data is always required to determine the root cause of being on track or off course. New business intelligence (BI) technology enables more affordable creation and delivery of dashboards.

Analyze results using BI tools. The ability for line managers to analyze worker performance data is very new. In the past, management has been dependent on the IT departments to design, create, test, and tune custom reports. Business intelligence tools are increasingly affordable and easy to use. Line managers can create ad hoc reports and drill down into supporting data on the fly and without IT intervention. The capability for HCSC stakeholders to analyze HCSC data is a critical success factor for any HCSC program.

Take action and manage the program of HCSCM work. Analysis of performance results will help to identify additional opportunities for improvement. Optimizing the HCSC will require a continuous stream of initiatives and each of these projects will yield additional ROI for the organization. It is important to have a program management capability in place to track and manage all HCSCM-related projects.

The Need for a HCSC Community

A community of supply chain stakeholders has developed and created an opportunity for companies to share their successes, lessons learned, and innovations. Supply chain associations and industry work groups continually work to advance SCM thinking. The result is that the entire SCM discipline advances globally. Founding innovators, such as Edward Deming and Taiichi Ohno, could never imagine how SCM would mature and improve over time. While we may not be able to foresee how HCSCM will be innovated and optimized as it matures, we can be sure that HCSCM will be a key factor in corporate success for decades to come. As the HCSC discipline develops it is important for HCSC stakeholders to establish a forum for sharing their experiences and innovations. You can start sharing your thoughts at www.HumanCapitalSupplyChain. com.

KEY POINTS: CRAFT THE BUSINESS CASE FOR HCSCM

- Start by crafting a conceptual business case, which will demonstrate the feasibility of the HCSCM program.

- The most important financial number needed to estimate for the business case is the total spend on human capital. This dollar figure will be an enormous proportion of the total revenues or total expenses. Just a small percentage savings will translate into massive real-dollar savings.

- Design the HCSCM program to fund the expensive, but necessary, automation efforts with the savings achieved through process and policy changes.

- Even though the ROI for implementing a HCSCM program is quick and substantial, it is often difficult to get it approved because the costs and benefits are spread across the organization.

- Most often, companies need the CEO to request and approve a conceptual business case for HCSCM in order to mobilize this strategic, cross-functional initiative.

- KPIs and benchmarking data can be used to develop additional qualitative details about the ROI.

- Once KPIs are selected, and after baseline, current performance, and benchmarking data is gathered, it is then possible to set achievable and measurable goals for the HCSCM program.

- Establishing performance management processes helps focus the whole HCSC on achieving the goals. To achieve those goals and prove ROI, HCSC technology must continuously measure, track, and report performance.

Chapter 4: Wrap Your Arms Around the Total Cost of Human Capital

CHAPTER OBJECTIVES:

- Convince the CFO to calculate the company's total human capital spend.

- Provide methods to ballpark the human capital spend.

- Provide guidance on how to conduct a bottom-up calculation of human capital spend.

CFO CALL TO ACTION

CFOs are responsible for managing total corporate spending patterns. Knowing a firm's total human capital spend is mandatory and imperative in a highly competitive market. Because many CFOs lack visibility inside the overall cost of human capital throughout the company, they may not appreciate the magnitude of the spend or the missed opportunities to reduce costs and increase revenues.

CFOs must assign their procurement and accounting resources to research and calculate the company's total cost of human capital. Once an accurate picture of the data exists, the CFO can better understand the options and implement improved business practices, processes, and technologies to track this critical number on an ongoing basis.

Even more fundamental than these operational improvements, CFOs must restructure the way financial and management data is reported in order to separate people costs from non-people costs so that the cost can be managed on a routine basis. That is, financial statements have to reflect the true importance and total cost of human capital to the organization.

ESTIMATING TOTAL HUMAN CAPITAL SPEND: THE BACK OF THE ENVELOPE APPROACH

Total human capital spend requires knowledge of the direct *and* indirect human capital costs. Direct human capital costs are easily captured through internal systems (e.g. HRIS, payroll system), but estimating and capturing indirect human capital costs can be quite complex.

As another check and balance, both the costs of the directly payrolled workforce and the workforce paid through accounts payable must be combined to grasp the total cost of human capital. Companies often focus too much on the costs associated with their direct workforce and are not as vigilant about tracking and managing the cost of their indirect workforce.

Unfortunately, procurement departments typically lump human capital spend in with the broader category of their services spend. Service spend is wide-ranging and includes marketing, print, travel, telecom, facilities, and legal services in addition to temporary, contractor, consulting, and business process outsourcing spend. Isolating human capital spend from services spend is difficult.

Payment Method

Workforce Type	Direct	Indirect
Permanent	Full & Part Time Employees	PEO
Flexible	Contractors	Temps, Contractors, Consultants, Business Services, Outsourcers

**Figure 1: Direct and indirect human capital costs
must be combined.**

Because organizations have such limited visibility into their indirect human capital spend and so little research has been conducted, there is no benchmark data that provides a good estimate of the percentage of the services spend that is considered indirect human capital spend.

Companies that have implemented vendor management services programs may have a handle on their actual indirect labor spend, but additional financial analysis is required to get a full picture of total human capital spend. Depending on the type of business, and based on the financial analysis, indirect human capital spend is likely to be ten times the temporary labor spend.

Even with, "back of the envelope" calculations a company's indirect spend on labor-based categories is a meaningful proportion of the organization's total purchases. That is reason enough to manage human capital spend more tightly but the potential for savings is staggering. This is also an opportunity for procurement to broaden their focus from goods management to include service management in a more accelerated or dramatic way to achieve significant savings.

ESTIMATING TOTAL HUMAN CAPITAL SPEND: THE BOTTOM-UP APPROACH

Even if data about average human capital spend were more readily available, each enterprise needs to capture their actual human capital spend, and a bottom-up approach is required.

Worker Type

Companies must understand the cost of all of the types of human capital they utilize. When managing labor spend, companies have traditionally focused on the cost of their direct, full-time workforce. Vendor management services programs have helped companies monitor and manage a greater portion of their temporary labor spend and it is increasingly common for firms to push consulting spend through their VMS. Getting visibility into total human capital spend means planning and tracking spend across all worker types. We have identified six main worker-type categories:

Direct Labor. For most firms, direct labor is the most expensive cost of doing business. Direct labor includes all full- and part-time resources employed by the firm. These employees may work on-site, off-site, at home, or offshore. The firm is the employer of record for direct labor and these employees all receive a W-2 directly from the firm. Data about the spend on direct labor can be found in the HRIS, payroll, and accounting systems.

Starting in the 1990s, professional employment organizations (PEOs) were formed. If a PEO is used to manage part or all of a workforce, that PEO is the legal and direct employer (i.e. generates the employees W-2).

Temporary Labor. Temporary labor includes those workers employed through staffing firms. Temporary labor is typically paid by the hour but can also be paid by the piece, shift, or day. Temporary workers may offer their skills to the firm for just a few hours up to a few years.

In general, the staffing firm is the employer of record for the temporary labor and generates the W-2s. Sometimes staffing firms can staff workers from other companies (e.g. other staffing firms) and so they may have a corp-to-corp relationship from the talent's employing staffing firm.

Staffing firms typically generate a weekly, biweekly, bimonthly, or monthly invoice and send it to the accounts payable department for payment. Firms with tens of millions or more in annual temporary spend have increasingly utilized vendor management systems to track contingent labor spend. Data about the spend on temporary labor is kept in the accounts payable and VMS systems.

Independent Contractors. Independent contractors are self-employed workers. If they have a business license they will engage in a corp-to-corp relationship with the firm, but if they don't, the company pays their invoices through accounts payable and processes a 1099 at the end of the year. This worker type creates co-employment risk for firms, and close monitoring of independent contracts is a standard business practice. Independent contractors are responsible for paying their own employer side taxes and benefits. Data about the contractor spend is kept in the accounts payable system.

Consultants. Professional services are generally hired on a project basis and provide specialized or niche expertise to an enterprise. Consulting projects are typically awarded to the firm that wins the evaluation process. The evaluation process typically includes the comparison of multiple vendors through requests for information (RFI), requests for proposal (RFP) and requests for quote (RFQ). The final result is a statement of work (SOW), and a services agreement, which includes agreed-upon milestones, payments, and terms. The consulting firm invoices the firm at the agreed milestone and the payment is processed through accounts payable. Data about the spend on consulting services labor is kept in the accounts payable system.

Business Services Providers. Business services are those services provided by niche experts such as attorneys, accountants, and marketing and PR professionals. These types of services are typically charged on an hourly, retainer, or project basis, and the typical expectation is that the company will have an ongoing relationship with these vendors. Spend on business service providers is easily overlooked. The service provider invoices the firm at the agreed-upon milestone and payment is processed through accounts payable. Data about the spend on business services is found in the accounts payable system.

Outsourced Services. Finance and accounting, human resources, payroll and benefits, recruitment, customer support, manufacturing, procurement, and IT are examples of functions that are commonly carried out by outside firms. Business process outsourcing (BPO) firms have multi-year contracts that include service level agreements (SLAs), which typically include volume and performance-based fee scales. BPO providers commonly deliver their services from offshore locations. The BPO firm invoices the customer firm at the agreed-upon milestone, and the payment is processed through accounts payable. Data about the spend on outsourced services labor is found in the accounts payable system.

The complexity of this analysis depends heavily on how quickly and thoroughly the company is able to isolate each and every spending category, so the human capital costs need to be well coded. It's important to understand the various taxes, benefits, assets, and other costs associated with each worker and worker type for a total human capital spend analysis.

Skill set reach

The initial target for human capital spend managers are those skill sets that are both 1) frequently filled through external suppliers and 2) higher-paid positions. Since IT positions meet both those criteria, it makes sense that IT is among the first departments to be analyzed. Luckily, IT is often the fastest adopter of VMS technology, so it may be easier to gather the necessary data.

Light industrial and commercial staffing have been slow to adopt VMS because of the low bill rates, unique requirements, and smaller perceived opportunities for savings. While some skill sets have been a common target for spend management, spend management is permeating all types of skill sets.

Business unit reach

Some organizational units may have more visibility into their human capital spend than others. Typically firms that utilize a VMS rollout the program in a small portion of their business (e.g. one department in a single business unit) and expand from there.

Geographic reach

VMS programs have been a key enabler to human capital spend management. The first VMS was developed in the U.S. in the late 1990s. Although there has been an acceleration in VMS usage, adoption of VMS in the U.S. has been slow and global adoption even slower. It is common for firms to adopt VMS in their U.S. operations and then deploy the VMS internationally in the following order: Europe, Asia Pac, then Latin America.

Capturing global spend is tricky because multiple currencies must be supported and exchange rates fluctuate continually. Further, employment costs vary widely by country, making it difficult to capture all labor-related costs.

Labor-based service categories only

Filtering out the labor-based categories from the broader set of services categories can be difficult. Some categories, such as temporary spend or professional services spend are more obvious. Business services spend, such as legal and accounting, can be more difficult to catch because they are not traditionally considered as labor spend. Some categories may require separating the people costs from the non-people costs, such as travel, telecom, and facilities. For example, a portion of the marketing spend may be to a public relations agency for services (labor spend) but may also include printing fees for marketing collateral (non-labor spend).

All labor and related costs

The goal of the human capital spend analysis is to capture both total human capital spend and to be able to determine which types of labor are most cost effective for the enterprise. In order to make apples-to-apples comparisons across worker types, and conduct what-if workforce planning scenarios, all of the associated costs of employment must be captured. Non-wage costs include federal, state, and local taxes, worker's compensation, health and dental benefits, insurance, bonuses and commissions, agency fees, recruiter budgets, payroll processing fees, and so on.

Build on a solid starting point.

Most companies that have started a human capital spend management program implemented it in a limited portion of their business. The following diagram shows the typical scope of new human capital spend management programs relative to the overall potential:

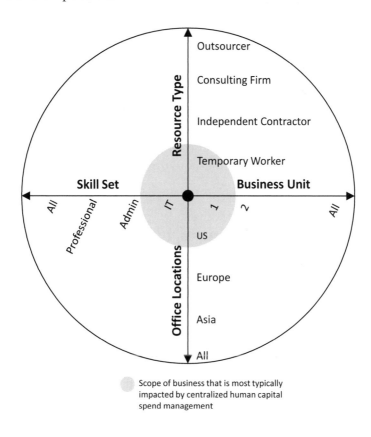

Scope of business that is most typically impacted by centralized human capital spend management

Figure 2: Typical scope of human capital spend management program

Prioritize efforts.

In addition to understanding total cost by category it is important to understand where there is the most spend and which categories can be impacted the most.

COMMON PITFALLS IN CAPTURING TOTAL HUMAN CAPITAL SPEND

If the bulk of this data is available in existing, internal systems, why is it so difficult to have full visibility into total human capital spend?

First of all, all the vendors must be coded correctly in the systems to be able to quickly find them. Secondly, data must be pulled out manually from multiple systems and massaged so that it can be merged. Thirdly, each worker type has different burdens (e.g. tax implications) by location, business unit, etc. Arriving at a reasonably accurate understanding of the total human capital spend using a bottom-up approach might be tedious and time-consuming until the process is routinized and automated.

NOW THAT WE KNOW THE NUMBERS, IT'S TIME TO GET TO WORK

Now that we've wrapped our arms around total human capital spend across the organization, including all labor categories and all relevant labor-related expenses, what do we do now?

The fact is that we've captured the data for a single point in time. It's possible to compare total human capital spend as a percent of revenues to competitors, but there is no ability to trap and monitor these costs on an ongoing basis. Having figured out the existing data sources and data quality issues we can now understand the need for additional business practices, reports, and technologies to support the efforts on an ongoing basis. But, the key outcome of this process is that, for the first time ever, we have a realistic peek at the total human capital spend.

KEY POINTS: ARMS AROUND TOTAL HC SPEND

- It is the CFO's responsibility to have a team determine the company's total human capital spend.

- "Back of the envelope" calculations show that a company's spend on labor-based categories is a meaningful proportion of the organization's total purchases and that the potential for savings is staggering.

- Capturing human capital spend is not easy and requires tedious data collection across the organization and databases.

- Once the total human capital spend at a single point in time is known, put business practices, processes, and technology in place to track and manage this spend on an ongoing basis.

Chapter 5: Engage the Stakeholders

CHAPTER OBJECTIVES:

- Identify key stakeholders within the organization and across the supply chain.

- Explain how to overcome the deep-rooted resistance to change.

- Explain why C-level leadership is a critical HCSC success factor.

- Describe how each stakeholder's role must change.

OVERCOMING THE CULTURE CLASH

A successful HCSC program is reliant upon hiring managers, HR, procurement, and staffing suppliers all working in concert with a shared set of goals and objectives. For most companies, this vision sounds like the impossible dream. Each of these groups has their own distinctive personality, culture, language, and view on human capital.

The HR department is known for being concerned about the softer side of people and ensures their health and happiness while on the job. HR has traditionally focused on the art of employee performance and satisfaction. HR struggles with being taken more seriously and has been making a great effort to evolve the HR function so that HR has a more strategic role within the organization. For decades, one of HR's most critical roles has been to be the worker's advocate, but their approach has tended to be all heart and paper-pushing and not as strategically and fiscally minded.

Procurement has traditionally focused on the management of goods, not services or human capital. Procurement has been hesitant to apply their skills to labor-related categories of spend. Certainly, procuring people is different than procuring goods, but a number of procurement's cost-saving principles can be successfully leveraged. Where HR may be considered more of an art, procurement and finance are seen as more of a science. With their intense focus on reducing price and optimizing terms, procurement's approach to managing human capital can be viewed as cost effective, but heartless.

Asking HR and procurement to work together may seem like mixing oil and water. For starters, they don't speak the same human capital language. HR uses terms like talent, recruitment, compensation, and benefits. Whereas, procurement uses terms like services procurement, labor-based categories, labor-related spend, spend under management, and cost containment. These different languages are a reflection of their different views on human capital.

Staffing suppliers operate in yet another world. While HR is considered a cost center within their own organizations, recruiters are the revenue generators in the staffing firm. Staffing firm recruiters speak the language of gross margin and mark-up and must manage customer and candidate satisfaction simultaneously to ensure a successful and profitable placement. Because staffing is their core business, the most successful firms are more metrics and performance oriented than the typical HR department. At their core, recruiters are sales people, selling to clients on one side of the desk and candidates on the other. At the same time their operations must be profitable, so staffing firms must also think like procurement. Staffing firms have to be skilled at both the people and the financial sides of their business. Perhaps they represent what an optimized blend between HR and procurement strengths looks like.

In the past, HR, procurement, and staffing suppliers have not worked together in a tightly coordinated and orchestrated way. Certainly, much business has been conducted, but the idea of highly structured HCSCs with distinct roles and responsibilities, with hard-and-fast service level agreements at hand-offs, and with the C-level sponsor at the helm, is a new and evolving concept.

As we've seen with manufacturing supply chains, those organizations that form, develop, manage, and mature their supply chains reap the highest quality results at the best possible price.

A well-running HCSC depends on HR, procurement, and staffing suppliers working together to deliver the right skills to the right location at the right time at the optimal price. Supply chain stakeholders must overcome the HR / procurement / supplier culture clash and leverage each other's strengths, personalities, and skill sets.

FEAR OF THE PERSON-WIDGET

What is really holding HR and procurement back from working in unison to drive their HCSC?

Resistance to change. From the HR point of view, people are human beings. Though it sounds silly to say it like that, HR fears that a HCSC sounds a bit too much like an assembly line. Even the term "human capital" appears to somehow minimize the "human" part. HR is concerned that the organization will overdevelop the analytical and scientific approach to human capital management, while procurement has the opposite concern.

Establishing a HCSC requires HR and procurement to both put aside their fears and sensitivities. HR must trust that the organization is not going to treat people as widgets; that's just not a sound long-term management practice. Procurement must recognize that they can leverage their goods procurement experience, but must also adjust their approach to address the uniqueness of people and teams. It makes good business sense to apply the same sound financial management to the planning and procurement of your workforce that you do in all of the other aspects of your business.

EXECUTIVE SPONSORSHIP IS THE CRITICAL CHANGE CATALYST

At the end of the day, the only impetus for HR, procurement, and hiring managers to work together in unison is a directive from the executive suite. The culture shift is just too big to overcome without C-level sponsorship and drive.

The figure, below, illustrates how each key stakeholder has worthy, stand-alone human capital goals, but it is a top-down executive-level directive that creates the ability for HR, procurement, and hiring managers to work together and interweave their objectives to achieve a common strategic result.

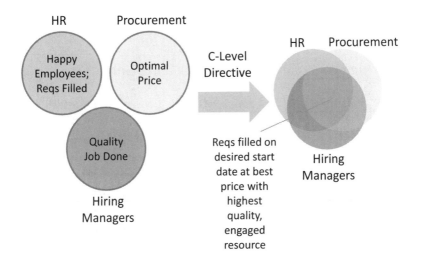

Figure 3: Key Stakeholders Working in Concert Yields Strategic Outcome

Executives are the key to change management: the VMS Example

As we've seen with vendor management system adoption across the country, an executive sponsor and a program evangelist are needed to muster and maintain momentum around VMS implementation and usage. Without this level of support, a VMS project will have great difficulty getting off the ground. VMS programs that happen to launch without this level of support may get rolling, but the cost savings and supplier management opportunity is never maximized.

In addition to the compelling year-one cost savings associated with VMS, the projects require little capital investment and are low risk, yet VMS adoption rates remain relatively low. Case study upon case study has shown that implementing a VMS will reduce contingent labor costs by five to twenty percent or more, which represents tens of millions of dollars saved by large corporations. VMS software and services have matured, making implementations relatively quick and painless.

With a measured upside and manageable downside, it's surprising that the VMS adoption rate is so low. The hard dollar savings do not seem to provide companies with enough motivation to kick off their VMS projects.

Success of a VMS program often depends on two key inputs: a single, self-appointed VMS champion within the organization, and executive sponsorship.

Without a day-to-day leader, the level of complexity and coordination can easily grind any forward momentum to a standstill. Even with an evangelist in place, VMS initiatives struggle.

Because VMS programs depend on so many disparate organizations working together (HR, procurement, IT, hiring managers, staffing suppliers) executive sponsorship is mandatory. Key departments report up through various C-levels, making it necessary to drive the priority of the VMS project from the top down.

American industry has taken a long time to learn the importance of C-level support for VMS programs, but we have yet to find ways to educate C-levels of the business case and benefits of VMS adoption.

The human capital supply chain depends on a similar set of diverse stakeholders, making C-level support the most critical success factor for any HCSC program.

Management Stakeholders Drive Real Results

HCSC leaders are responsible for successfully building the supply chain function. HCSC stakeholders must be the change agents that transform a siloed and disconnected supply chain into an efficient, interconnected operation. While executives must initially shift corporate focus to HCSC optimization, all of the supply chain stakeholders must work together each and every day to make the supply chain optimally efficient.

Manufacturing supply chains had a similar set of stakeholders during the 1980s. Renowned efficiency expert Edward Deming armed management with new tools and techniques, like continuous improvement. People drive the supply chain, and the people are responsible for its smooth functioning and performance improvements, one small change at a time.

Sample Human Capital Stakeholder Chain

The diagram below shows a single combination of stakeholders that make up a HCSC. This highly simplified stakeholder supply chain utilizes a staffing supplier to deliver new, temporary talent to the hiring manager via a staffing program office. This model assumes that the decision to hire talent from outside the company (rather than using existing internal talent) has already been made.

Figure 4: Illustrative Human Capital Stakeholder Chain

In our illustration, the staffing program office is run by the procurement department. However, some companies hand this responsibility over to HR or outsource it to a staffing supplier partner. There has been a trend toward vendor-neutral program offices, meaning no vendor is favored in the staffing process. Staffing firms often refer to this type of service as a managed service program (MSP). There are also non-neutral arrangements (e.g. master vendor) wherein the staffing firm running the program office manages sub-vendors to fill only those orders that they choose not to fill themselves. While some companies might view a non-neutral program office as dangerous because it gives too much control to a single vendor, others believe this to be a strategic supplier relationship that results in the best cost/quality outcome.

Additionally, in our example, HR is responsible for the onboarding of the temporary worker. In some firms, especially where temporary labor is viewed as expendable, procurement may take on these roles.

The hiring manager takes over the management role, ensuring that workers receive feedback about their performance and appropriate information about completing their time cards.

As can be seen from our example, there are many high-level stakeholder roles and responsibilities that must be determined for a HCSC. High-level stakeholder supply chains must be developed based on worker type (e.g. temporary, contractor, consultant), geography, skill set, etc. While the stakeholder supply chains are clearly oversimplified versions of how a supply chain functions, they provide a high-level context that clarifies key stakeholder relationships and responsibilities.

New Roles and Responsibilities Required

Each stakeholder's role changes with the implementation of a HCSC. The remainder of this chapter explains the changes required, role by role.

Executive Stakeholders

The CEO, CFO, and COO are responsible for defining a company's business strategy and goals, but the strategies and plans of any organization are reliant on the talent that executes them. While the executive stakeholders do not drive the company on a day-to-day basis, they are responsible for the forward momentum of the corporate financial gear that fires up the HCSC. In economic downturns, executives will slow or reverse the flow of the HCSC through mass layoffs. As we've stressed, it is imperative that a C-level executive sponsors the HCSC initiative.

CEO. CEOs have only begun to focus on the strategic nature of human capital. In our knowledge economy, the cost of talent has become the greatest expense for CEOs, but has drawn too little of their attention. CEOs need to optimize the cost and value of their human capital not only to remain competitive, but to remain in business. Clearly, CEOs cannot afford to have a hands-off approach to HR.

CEOs have been driving cost out of nearly every aspect of their business through automation, outsourcing, and offshoring. CEOs need to also apply these techniques to talent acquisition and talent management. The CEO has to look at how to build a more innovative, productive, and cost-effective total workforce. A natural next step is for CEOs to manage their permanent and flexible workforces holistically, and to establish and manage an efficient HCSC.

In the 1970s the chief executive was concerned about automating the financial management of their organization. In the 1980s they automated manufacturing, and in the 1990s the sales and customer management functions. By 2009 the customer interaction was automated and pushed to the Internet. CEOs now need to look to new areas of automation, such as HCSC automation, in order to dramatically reduce costs.

The U.S. workforce has transitioned from a manufacturing to a knowledge workforce. The knowledge workforce possesses more highly paid skill sets. A knowledge worker has much more financial impact on the corporation, is difficult to manage, and the cost of recruitment and retention is higher than in prior eras. CEOs' largest expenditure used to be equipment and raw materials. Now, the CEO's largest cost is most often labor. We estimate that wages and labor-related costs for the average U.S. company make up twenty-five to seventy-five percent of a company's expenses. CEOs and their boards are taking a closer look at the cost of talent and trying to find out how to reduce the overall costs to their organization.

The recession in the first decade of the new century resulted in massive, worldwide layoffs. As the global economy moves toward recovery, CEOs will rebuild their businesses and begin rehiring. Strategic CEOs streamline and automate their HCSC in advance to be able to hire quality talent faster and more inexpensively than in the past.

For those who do not make these fundamental and necessary HCSC changes, rehiring simply magnifies their poor processes and systems. In addition to the high cost of their outdated approach, these CEOs experience poor results and lose the best talent to competing firms. Most importantly, companies positioned to quickly hire quality talent can grow revenues the fastest.

CFO. CFOs have the responsibility of keeping a company's revenues growing and costs under control. When it comes to human capital, CFOs have focused on setting compensation and making big-ticket decisions like outsourcing, offshoring, and layoffs. Several understand the financial benefits of VMS programs and support their implementation. Even though CFOs are responsible for the quantitative management of talent costs, most CFOs have not demanded responsibility for managing the firm's total cost of human capital; if they did, they would most certainly be pushing for the financial optimization of their HCSC.

One might think that the biggest financial expense of the company being labor and labor-related costs, human capital management might top the CFO's agenda. "Analytical and precise by nature, CFOs are famously averse to anything that can be deemed 'squishy,'" explains Scott Leibs, executive editor of *CFO Magazine*.[1] "Subjectivity, vagueness, wiggle room, these are qualities that CFOs routinely attempt to expunge from budgets, briefings, and business plans. They seek clarity as relentlessly as Sidewinder missiles seek heat, and that's generally to their credit. That may be one reason why many tend to regard 'human capital' as a euphemism for 'personnel' or 'labor' rather than a legitimate strategic issue. It's not that CFOs don't regard the collective capabilities of their workforces as critically important — they simply aren't sure what they're supposed to do about it. As a result, many leave the 'soft' side of human capital to the human-resources department and fixate on the salary, benefits, and other costs associated with all those bodies."

Just as HR departments started to care about wellness when healthcare costs skyrocketed, CFOs must now focus more attention on managing human capital and driving the HCSC. CFOs have to accelerate their efforts to understand the total cost of human capital, that is, the cost of both their permanent and flexible labor pools and all of the associated expenses. CFOs must lead the effort to develop and support decisions and strategic workforce plans that provide the firm with the best possible human capital at the lowest possible cost to the organization. In a global knowledge economy, CFOs must immediately become engaged and apply their skills to human capital management or they will quickly find their revenue growth constrained by a poor-functioning HCSC.

COO. The COO manages the organization's talent and hopes to employ the best people with the right fits. The HR industry has gone to great effort to assess the quality of talent. Personality and behavioral assessments, background checks, skill tests, and the like have become the means for determining candidate quality; but performance issues, high turnover, and low productivity are common quality issues within organizations. Perhaps, if banking COOs had been more involved in defining and monitoring their hiring processes, some of the financial industry ethical woes could have been avoided. Ensuring the quality of talent has become paramount.

VP of HR

HR is traditionally responsible for payroll, benefits, compensation, career planning and development, training, recruitment, and workforce planning. HR has been working on getting a seat at the executive table, but most heads of HR still fill a VP rather than a C-level role.

The VP of HR is responsible for determining the talent requirements necessary to support the business strategy, goals, and plan. The VP of HR translates the financial goals of the business into talent goals, which means they own the workforce planning portion of the HCSC. Workforce planning is a relatively underdeveloped discipline within most organizations, and is one of the least automated or understood processes.

In theory, the workforce plan determines whether and when additional resources are needed. The talent needs must be understood by skill, location, and timing. Knowing when and where skill sets are needed is only the first step. The VP of HR must also support insource/outsource decisions and determine the optimal talent mix. Full-time, part-time, contractors, consultants, and temps all offer various value to the organization and the VP of HR must work with procurement to determine the best talent mix based on resource cost and scarcity, as well as the length of time the skill is needed. The VP of HR develops the talent acquisition plan and reports to the executive team (CEO, COO, CFO) on progress toward the plan.

HR also manages internal talent levels and develops the permanent workforce. In most cases, direct employees make up the bulk of a company's worker base because that tends to be the most cost-effective approach, and worker motivations are aligned most tightly with the company. HR is responsible for all aspects of talent management, including internal mobility, as direct employees are the most readily available resources and, by definition, the most highly invested talent pool.

In the past, HR tended to conduct workforce planning exercises annually, or when required, and tracked them on a monthly basis. When data collection is mostly a manual exercise, it is difficult to tally the information more frequently. The manufacturing supply chain shifted from a monthly production mentality in the '70s to a daily and even hourly order level review by the end of the '80s. HR has to make that same leap to the daily tuning and management of staffing levels. Staffing firms already think this way. With the advent of world-class manufacturing techniques in the '80s, the only way for HR to enable constant daily workforce planning is through automation of the entire workforce planning process.

The VP of HR manages the recruitment team to source and fill any talent gaps. Depending on the organization, HR may also be responsible for acquisition and management of the flexible workforce as well.

Head of Procurement

The procurement department within organizations has traditionally focused on the process of strategizing, planning, sourcing, and purchasing goods, not services. Procurement departments have started to shift from goods to services, such as mobile phone services and travel services, but few have jumped wholeheartedly into the procurement of people.

The procurement of human capital is quite different from the procurement of goods and services, and the head of procurement needs to lead the charge. The head of procurement needs to drive change within their own department, since both new skills sets and procurement processes are needed to create and manage labor-based categories of spend and the HCSC. In addition, the head of procurement must be an evangelist for HCSC throughout the organization. Procurement has to educate hiring managers on the benefits of the HCSC so that they are able to align with HR and take on the responsibility of establishing, managing, measuring, and optimizing the HCSC on a day-to-day basis.

Head of Recruitment

The head of recruitment must acquire talent to fulfill the workforce plan. The head of recruitment is responsible for hiring the best talent at the best price, at the right time and location. In order to fill the position, they must work with the hiring manager and their team until the placement is made.

Recruitment departments tend to focus on direct and permanent hires. If no direct hire is made fast enough, recruiters then may look to other talent sources, such as staffing firms. In the HCSC-driven world, recruiters have to be more sophisticated and cost-effective. For example, they must consider all worker types (e.g. temps, contractors, and consultants) before getting started on a new requisition in order to fill positions without wasting time and money on multiple searches.

Recruitment process outsourcing (RPO) is an interesting and growing model in that organizations are outsourcing all or part of the recruiting function in order to reduce costs and improve recruitment performance.

In addition to hiring the talent, the recruitment team is most often responsible for ensuring the smooth onboarding of new talent into the organization and into their new positions, so that the workers are productive as quickly as possible.

Head of IT

Corporate IT tends to organize around departments, but the HCSC requires a seamless, end-to-end automated business process across finance, HR, procurement, and staffing supplier systems. IT departments need to be organized to accommodate cross-functional, cross-business units, and cross-company goals, which means that one, overall IT owner for HCSC automation makes sense.

Staffing Suppliers

Many staffing firms believe their role and value-add is to find suitable candidates faster than their clients can. Unfortunately this mentality positions staffing firms as tactical suppliers to hiring companies. Staffing firms have great difficulty differentiating themselves in the marketplace and are often considered a commodity service rather than a strategic staffing partner.

Staffing firms establish a duplicate recruitment infrastructure when compared to hiring companies. Obviously, hiring companies fund the HCSC, so a duplicate infrastructure means that companies end up paying for two full sets of recruitment processes, people, and technologies. Staffing firms have tended to be a company's back-up plan in case talent cannot be found directly. Duplication doubles costs and HCSC optimization will push as much cost out of the process as possible.

With accelerated adoption of outsourcing business functions to staffing firms, the staffing suppliers have a much more integrated relationship with companies. Strategic staffing suppliers must form more exclusive, closer-knit, performance-based, and longer-term relationships with their clients. Many commodity providers rely on their relationship with clients and use this personal relationship as their primary differentiator. As hiring companies form long-term relationships with firms that consistently deliver talent at the best price, personal relationships will be a less meaningful differentiator.

At the same time, hiring companies are asking more from their staffing suppliers. Hiring firms are pushing additional HR functions to their staffing suppliers, such as background checks and onboarding paperwork. At some point, hiring companies may require that staffing firms go a step further and provide healthcare benefits, which would clearly maximize the client's hiring flexibility. The staffing firm's role is obviously broadening.

Staffing firms have tried to become strategic partners to their clients. This has been a difficult shift for most firms as their comfort zone has been transactionally-oriented staffing. One way for staffing suppliers to have a more strategic role is to participate in the workforce planning process with their clients. Further, staffing firms that help corporations implement HCSC have much to gain as they can transition their existing trusted relationships into truly strategic ones, which will differentiate them from the masses of commodity staffing suppliers and create a strategic competitive advantage.

Another potential differentiator for staffing suppliers in the HCSC world is to become the staffing firm of choice for workers. The recruiter who has a trusted relationship with the talent will be best positioned to provide that talent to the hiring manger on a just-in-time basis. Since staffing firms represent multiple hiring companies, they are in an optimal position to be successful and profitable with this approach.

Staffing firms must stay ahead of their clients in terms of strategic staffing concepts like HCSC. Staffing firms do not remain relevant if they do not offer staffing capabilities, skills, processes, or technology that is beyond what hiring companies can do for themselves. As procurement takes a bigger role in staffing and HCSCs are put in place, staffing firms must do everything in their power to ensure they have the broadest, most exclusive, and most integrated relationship possible with their clients.

Training and Professional Development

When new skills are needed, the decision may be made to train existing resources rather than procure new outside talent — that is, build rather than buy the skill. In these cases the head of training must participate in constantly identifying and making new skills available to the organization. The corporate training team is responsible for providing this service to staff. Because the workforce is increasingly mobile and more likely to jump between employers, we can anticipate that companies will be more strategic about their training investments.

Supporting Service Providers

There are a variety of third-party service providers that offer technology-based services along the supply chain. Services provided include: job posting, job distributors, candidate sourcing, background checking, drug testing, assessments, payroll processing, benefits, tax updates, and tax filings.

These service providers offer point solutions that provide value-added information to the HCSC. In most cases, data is exchanged between the supporting service provider and the supply chain. There has been an uptick in the use of these third-party services and a lot more duplicate data entry has resulted.

In many cases, these service vendors compete on price more than on quality and service level, so relationships are considered replaceable or interchangeable. The biggest issue in the HCSC is that the data needed by the third party is usually exchanged manually. Due to the increase in transactions with these mostly commoditized third parties, we can expect to see a greater focus on automating the data exchange between them and the HCSC in order to reduce costs and to quickly change out vendors without the added cost and hassle of training.

Employees and Candidates

Workers have become increasingly independent from their employer and more loyal to themselves, changing the traditional employment relationship. The rise of the free agent has literally loosened the ties between workers and employers. In the past, direct (or permanent) full-time employment was the preferred and most common employment relationship. According to Staffing Industry Analysts, about two percent of the total workforce is employed through staffing suppliers and this percentage is expected to rise.[2]

In other countries this number reaches as high as four percent. One of the main reasons workers seek direct employment is to obtain employee benefits such as health insurance. Laws concerning benefits apply to hiring companies but do not yet apply to staffing firms, though many staffing firms do offer optional benefits for workers while they are employed.

With or without employee benefits, more workers enjoy free-agent status. Workers, especially professionals, are seeking temporary, independent contractor and consulting relationships with employers. With these looser ties, workers have more control over when and where they work and their length of service. In this economic era, worker loyalty is to themselves rather than to their employer, and this is especially true with younger workers.

Candidates enter the HCSC by applying directly to the hiring company or via staffing suppliers. The recruitment and hiring process is no longer entirely manual as much of the hiring process has shifted to the Internet. Candidates are expected to maintain online profiles and electronic resumes, and complete online applications. Employers and staffing firms have automated much of their interactions with candidates and pushed much of the data entry of candidate data directly to candidates.

At the same time, candidate's expectations of the hiring process have increased. Candidates want technology to keep them informed of where they are in the hiring process with real-time personalized interaction. They know technology can enable this interaction and they have come to expect it. They can leverage their social and professional networks to find out what it is like to be an employee of the hiring company and can reach into the company's employee base to get the real story through blogs. Technology has not only shifted the administrative burden of the hiring process to candidates, it has empowered candidates and employees to expect transparency into the organization and across the supply chain.

From a HCSC perspective, hiring companies can expect to have less control and influence over the hiring and termination of their workers. Retention is increasingly complex when workers do not feel tied to their employer. Employers can be expected to be more hesitant to invest in the development of their employees since there is less likelihood that they will get their return on their training investment. One could argue that between talent acquisition and talent management, talent acquisition has become the more critical business capability for any company.

While hiring companies are at the helm and fund the HCSC, we must not forget that the workers provide the human capital energy that powers the supply chain.

KEY POINTS: ENGAGE THE STAKEHOLDERS

- The HR/procurement culture clash must be overcome in order to successfully implement the HCSC.

- Implementing a HCSC requires all of the key stakeholder's roles to change and fear of change can prevent an organization from saving millions.

- C-level sponsorship is required in order to get a HCSC program off the ground.

- High-level stakeholder roles must be strategically defined and may vary depending on corporate strategy and by worker type, geography, business unit, etc.

Chapter 6: The Eight Steps of Human Capital Supply Chain Management

CHAPTER OBJECTIVES:

- Characterize what's different in the new era of HCSCM.
- Describe and detail the eight HCSCM Steps.
- Conduct a quick wellness check on your HCSCM processes.

How Does HCSCM Fit-in?

Design of HCSC business processes can begin only after the total human capital spend is understood and the stakeholders are on board. HCSC processes unify hiring managers, HR, procurement, finance, accounting, and staffing supplier processes that relate to the procurement of all worker types. Most companies have not defined their collection of suppliers and processes as such, but they already have a HCSC in place. But the key to having an effective and efficient HCSC is actively managing it!

In addition to executing HCSCM processes there will always be a number of performance improving projects running in parallel. For example, there may be a program of work metrics, like decreasing cost per fill. There will probably also be parallel initiatives aimed to drive cost savings, e.g. cut professional services spend by ten percent. These special initiatives will be run as separate projects outside of regular HCSCM processes. These special projects might also result in HCSCM process changes.

The processes documented in this book are intended as suggestions or starting points to help accelerate a new process design. Once there is ownership of HCSCM processes, they can be tailored to specific strategies and situations.

EIGHT HCSCM STEPS AT-A-GLANCE

It is quite difficult to develop a simplified process for a complex business situation. The figure, below, represents a cross-functional, holistic view of the HCSCM process.

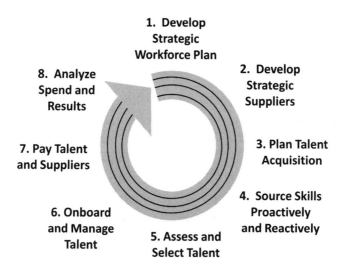

1. Develop Strategic Workforce Plan

8. Analyze Spend and Results

2. Develop Strategic Suppliers

7. Pay Talent and Suppliers

3. Plan Talent Acquisition

6. Onboard and Manage Talent

4. Source Skills Proactively and Reactively

5. Assess and Select Talent

Figure 5: The Holistic HCSCM Process

Eight HCSCM Steps	Brief Description
Develop Strategic Workforce Plan	Ensure the workforce enables the corporate strategy and annual business plan in the most efficient and effective way possible; size the total workforce needed (both permanent and flexible) and estimate specific skill surpluses and gaps; determine the optimal talent mix; make major staffing decisions (e.g. outsourcing, geographic migrations).
Develop Strategic Suppliers	Build strategic relationships with a few suppliers in order to maximize efficiency and minimize the cost of the HCSC.
Plan Talent Acquisition	Determine the ideal sourcing approach needed to fill each skill gap, considering all possible worker types (e.g. perm, temp, consultant, contractor).
Proactive and Reactive Skill Sourcing	Identify all of the suitable sources for active job orders and create and manage long-term talent pipelines.

Assess and Select Talent	Efficiently hire the talent that is the best fit at the best price for a specific job requisition or project.
Onboard and Manage Talent	Ramp up talent so they are performing at or better than expectations as quickly as possible.
Pay Talent and Suppliers	Provide accurate and timely payment for services rendered and be in compliance of all supplier contracts.
Analyze Human Capital Spend and Results	Achieve one hundred percent visibility into human capital spend across all global divisions and analyze actual workforce performance as compared to expectations.

CHARACTERISTICS OF THE EMERGING HCSCM PROCESS

Note the high-level differences between most HCSCM processes and the emerging ideal vision.

Figure 6: Traditional and Ideal HCSCM Process Characteristics

Traditional HCSCM Process	Ideal HCSCM Process
Siloed	Seamless
No single, end-to-end process owner	C-level ownership and accountability
Enables annual business plan	Strategic driver of business performance
Planned annually, measured monthly	Planned monthly, continually measured
Talent levels corrected reactively when there is a problem	Talent levels corrected proactively and routinely
Highly manual and paper based	Highly automated and paperless

Siloed vs. Seamless

Traditional HCSC management processes are siloed in so many ways; strong executive leadership is required to knock down these walls. Companies need to conduct deeper due diligence on their suppliers and develop strategic relationships, eliminating intra-company silos, so that supply chain costs can be jointly reduced. Breaking down departmental silos requires a transformation of HCSCM practices and C-level support. We often find different work practices and processes by worker type. Most commonly, HR focused on direct hires and procurement supported contingent workforce management. It is critical for companies to break down this silo so that key stakeholders have total visibility into their staffing options. The HCSCM process should be seamless across companies and their suppliers, as well as across departments, worker types, and geographies.

Many vs. One Overarching Owner

A single sponsor for the HCSC is required in order to overcome the variety of cultures and conflicting agendas along the supply chain. C-level ownership over the development, management, and refinement of the supply chain will deliver optimal results. While each silo could improve their operations, additional gains can be made when synergies across the supply chain are encouraged.

Enabling vs. Strategic Capability

Every company has a HCSC, by definition. That is, every firm has the capability to select, hire, onboard, manage, and pay talent; but described this way, talent management is only an enabling capability.

In our knowledge economy, creating and maintaining the best workforce is paramount to success. The HCSCM cycle must be honed into an efficient, productive, profit-generating machine. Human capital is a strategic differentiator for every firm, and the supply of that human capital must be managed strategically.

Infrequent vs. Continual Measurement

One of the key capabilities that enable continuous improvement in the manufacturing supply chain has been the availability of accurate performance data about the operations. Additionally, managers are expected to track, analyze, and act on performance fluctuations very quickly. In the past, managers acted on gut instinct or waited until the monthly report was released. Access to trusted real-time data enabled rapid and continuous improvement in product quality and cost.

There is a trend toward data-driven decisions all over the organization, including human capital management. Establishing a HCSC requires that corporations put a robust performance management capability in place for human capital management, and provide role-based access to up-to-date workforce performance data.

Massive Corrective Action vs. Routine Tuning

Workforce adjustments are often made on a reactive basis as a corrective measure. Over- and underutilization is not caught early, and hiring (or separation) plans are accelerated after market conditions change, rather than before. Major workforce corrections are required because issues are detected too late.

With the continual review of productivity against business performance, companies will have real-time insight into staffing needs and can be well positioned to make small and continual corrections to their staffing levels.

Manual vs. Automated Processes

There are a number of complex systems that need to be connected in order to automate the HCSC. Without integration, duplicate data entry is rampant, which is costly and time consuming. Software development technologies and approaches make it easier than ever for systems to exchange data.

Corporations have been giving lip service to enabling the paperless office for decades. The new HCSC process permits e-signatures and reduces the amount of printed documentation through the use of web forms and workflow automation.

New functionality, applications, and online tools (e.g. strategic workforce planning tools) reduce the dependence on Excel spreadsheets and standalone documents. For maximum efficiency financial, accounting, procurement, HR, and supplier systems need to be integrated from one end of the supply chain to the other.

HCSCM PROCESSES DEFINED

As we've stressed, formalizing HCSC and defining HCSC management processes is the foundation of any HCSC program. Without a formalized HCSCM program a company will not be in a position to systematically remove costs and maintain performance benefits.

Another essential is to document the unique business process; many companies skip this step because they find it tedious. The most common excuse heard is that the process changes too quickly to make documentation worthwhile. The end-to-end process must be documented in order to ensure that all the workflows actually do connect, everyone's roles are clearly defined, and hand-offs are well understood.Manufacturing firms are infamous for their ISO certified processes and HCSCs should adopt the same level of process discipline.

Step 1: Develop Strategic Workforce Plan

PROCESS OBJECTIVES

- Ensure the workforce plan enables the corporate strategy and annual business plan in the most efficient and effective way possible.
- Size the total workforce needed (both permanent and flexible) with estimated specific skill surpluses and gaps.
- Determine the optimal talent mix.
- Make major staffing decisions (e.g. outsourcing, geographic migrations).

PROCESS OWNER

CEO

OTHER KEY STAKEHOLDERS

COO, CFO, head of HR, business unit heads, head of recruitment, head of procurement

KEY ACTIVITIES

- Review corporate strategy and plan.
- Articulate the contribution and impact of human capital fluctuations and talent shortages on the top and bottom line as well as customer satisfaction.
- Develop or document the company's human capital key principles.

- Review the latest Human Capital Spend Analysis (an output from Step 8: Analyze Human Capital Spend and Results).

- Understand total human capital spend as well as spend by category.

- Verify that labor-based spend is grouped into meaningful categories for tracking and management.

- Develop management strategy and goals for each category of human capital spend.

- Determine optimal talent mix and key drivers so that underlying principles are understood.

- Identify high-level human capital supply and demand goals, risks, issues, and anticipated events (e.g. mergers and acquisitions, desired talent geographic migration).

- Articulate strengths and weaknesses of existing human capital (HC).

- Identify HC strengthening initiatives.

- Document employment brand goals, key characteristics, and messaging.

- Map current HC to needed HC and identify gaps.

- Document the strategic workforce plan.

- Review plan monthly and update plan as needed.

- Review corporate strategy monthly and realign strategic workforce plan as needed.

Process Input

- Corporate strategy and annual business plan
- Latest human capital spend analysis, HCSC performance analysis and previous strategic workforce plan
- Current internal and external talent supply by skill and by market
- Strategic workforce plan from prior years or templates

Process Output

Strategic workforce plan (including optimal talent-mix percentages and estimated budgets)

Key Process Issues

- It can be difficult to get C-level support for a strategic workforce plan because HR does not have a seat at the executive table.
- HR does not have a history of being numbers-driven but HR is critical to this process. Strategic workforce planning represents a culture shift for HR and new skill sets are needed.
- This is a new and underdeveloped business process with few experts, case studies, or best practices.
- The current process is highly manual and reliant on data that is non-existent, inaccurate, or difficult to gather.
- The market is constantly shifting, making it difficult to proactively identify talent supply shortages.

Key metrics

Total human capital spend under management. Having all of the human capital spend for the entire company covered by the strategic plan is the goal.

Supporting technology

- Strategic workforce planning software
- HRIS
- A/P and payroll
- Technology-enabled salary data — e.g. nextSource PeopleTicker, Staffing Industry Analysts, salary.com, payscale.com, industry-, discipline-, and geographic-specific benchmarking studies

Step 2: Develop Strategic Suppliers

PROCESS OBJECTIVE

Build strategic relationships with a few suppliers in order to maximize efficiency and minimize the cost of the HCSC.

PROCESS OWNER

Procurement

OTHER KEY STAKEHOLDERS

Hiring managers, head of HR, head of recruitment, business unit heads

KEY ACTIVITIES

- Review the strategic workforce plan and identify human capital categories in which suppliers will be utilized.
- Determine the ideal supplier mix (e.g. global, national, niche) and develop supplier evaluation criteria.
- Identify all existing suppliers, understand their staffing capabilities, and review their past performance.
- Develop a vendor consolidation strategy and goals based on ROI, and then implement.

- Identify potential staffing suppliers (e.g. staffing firms, search agencies, consulting firms, contractors).

- Qualify, evaluate, select, and tier staffing partners, being sure to conduct deep due diligence (e.g. RFx, reference checks, financial review).

- Negotiate pricing, terms, and service-level agreements (SLAs).

- Establish supplier performance management process, identify key performance indicators and agree upon scorecard.

- Assign overall ownership of the supplier relationship to one person.

- Develop supplier relationship management and communication process.

- Develop and manage supplier performance improvement action plan including routine audits.

- Terminate supplier relationships that aren't working.

PROCESS INPUTS

- Strategic workforce plan
- Existing staffing suppliers across all worker types
- Supplier diversity goals

PROCESS OUTPUTS

- Signed supplier agreements and SLAs
- Rate cards
- Agreed upon supplier scorecards

- Suppliers are not aware of company's long-term goals and needs.

- It is difficult to consistently manage a large number of suppliers with limited resources.

- Companies tend to treat suppliers as a commodity and do not invest in developing deeper, strategic relationship. In order to lower the cost of talent they may make a short-sighted trade off with talent quality.

- Companies need to be highly selective when partnering with staffing suppliers. Partnering with those firms that are relentless about continuous improvement in terms of driving up talent quality while driving cost out of the HCSC is ideal.

- Due diligence on suppliers does not go deep enough. Since supplier costs are passed onto hiring companies in the form of mark-up, hiring firms need to be vigilant about ensuring their vendors and their vendor's vendors are operating at maximum efficiency.

- Supplier network and systems are not integrated with corporate systems.

- Some suppliers benefit from favoritism based on personal relationships, which is not in the company's best interest.

KEY METRICS

Supplier performance

SUPPORTING TECHNOLOGY

- VMS
- Procurement system
- Corporate ATS
- Accounting
- eRFx software
- Contract management software
- Supplier portal
- Supplier management software

Step 3: Plan Talent Acquisition

PROCESS OBJECTIVE

Determine the ideal sourcing approach needed to fill each skill gap, considering all possible worker types (e.g. perm, temp, contractor, and consultant).

PROCESS OWNER

VP of HR

KEY STAKEHOLDERS

Head of recruitment, CEO, CFO, COO, business unit heads, head of HR, head of procurement, hiring managers

KEY ACTIVITIES

- Review the strategic workforce plan.
- Identify needed skills, location, and timing of each skill gap.
- Articulate needs as job requisitions or projects, and document human capital requirements.
- Identify assumptions about how the economy and skill supply will impact time to fill and cost to fill.
- Adjust hiring needs based on turnover, succession plans, and time to full productivity.
- Calculate and enter expected time to fill.
- Enter human capital needs and costs into workforce planning model (e.g. may need more internal recruiters; may need to buy software).

- Review optimal talent mix and compare to current actual.
- Conduct what-if scenarios with various worker types (e.g. direct, temp, consultant, contractor) to determine ideal worker type mix.
- Determine desired worker type by requisition or project.
- Calculate desired start dates.
- Based on desired worker type and lead times, determine sourcing start dates (e.g. requisition approval date).
- Develop checkpoints and contingency plans for identifying and managing jeopardized start dates.
- Execute the plan.
- Track sourcing start dates for requisitions and projects.
- Confirm need, timing, job requirements, location, desired worker type, and compensation.
- Approve requisition/project.
- Manage the acquisition plan, track plan routinely, and review progress toward plan weekly.
- Conduct checkpoint meetings and trigger contingency plans if needed.
- Communicate the talent acquisition plan by sharing the plan with internal business units and key suppliers.
- Review plan weekly and update plan monthly.
- Review corporate strategy and strategic workforce plan monthly and realign talent acquisition plan weekly.

Process Input

- Latest human capital spend analysis, HCSC performance analysis, strategic workforce plan and prior talent acquisition plan
- Talent supply mix percentages, by skill and by market
- Salary as well as bill and pay-rate ranges by skill by market
- Data by skill, location, and worker type (data provided should be a range): time to fill (i.e. lead time to hire), time to full productivity, turnover, and succession plans.

Process Output

- Talent acquisition plan (updated monthly and additionally, as needed)
- Communications to hiring managers, staffing suppliers and other stakeholders

Key Process Issues

- Talent acquisition planning tends to be focused on the permanent workforce and the flexible workforce is an afterthought; the plan should cover all worker types (e.g. direct hires, temps, contractors, consultants).
- No matter what the ideal new-hire start date is, the majority of hiring is kicked off at the start of the year.
- Current plans do not typically factor in realistic timing for recruiting, hiring, and onboarding.
- Plans are reviewed and revised infrequently but should be living documents.

- Companies have new and underdeveloped business process with few best practices and experts.

- Just as with strategic workforce planning, talent acquisition planning is a highly manual process that is reliant on data that is non-existent, inaccurate, or difficult to gather.

KEY METRICS

There should be a handful of performance goals for the talent acquisition plan that the plan owner identifies, e.g. reduce cost of talent acquisition by twenty percent, increase use of outsourcing to reduce total human capital costs.

SUPPORTING TECHNOLOGY

- Strategic Workforce Planning software
- ATS
- HRIS

Step 4: Proactive and Reactive Skill Sourcing

PROCESS OBJECTIVE

Identify all of the suitable sources for active job orders, then create and manage long-term talent pipelines.

PROCESS OWNER

Head of recruitment

KEY STAKEHOLDERS

Business unit heads, hiring managers, head of HR

KEY ACTIVITIES

For reactive requisition filling:

- Receive notification of approved and open job requisitions.
- Assign requisition to recruiter.
- Prepare job posting.
- Design knock-out questions.
- Distribute posting to internal job board, career site, external job boards, networks, and VMS.
- Distribute posting to professional contacts and generate referrals.
- Search internal database of past applicants and candidates.
- Search internal database of current employees and employee alumni.

- Search job boards, other subscription-based and "public databases, social networks, and websites for candidates.

- Review internal applicants and all potential candidates.

- Contact suitable talent, conduct initial screenings, and assess interest and availability.

- Shortlist top candidates for further assessment.

For proactive candidate sourcing:

- Review strategic workforce plan and talent acquisition plan.

- Identify expected long-term skill shortages and high-turnover skill sets.

- Identify talent pools to be developed.

- Identify and source potential talent and assign to appropriate pool.

- Write talent pool communication plan and execute to plan.

PROCESS INPUT

Approved requisitions and projects

PROCESS OUTPUT

- Top candidates by position
- Engaged talent pools

Key process issues

- There is no shared skill taxonomy across the supply chain, so searching for qualified resources requires multiple and complex keyword and other advanced searches.

- The identification of top candidates is typically a manual, subjective, and time-consuming review of resumes and proposals.

- Recruiters tend to have a preference to invest in new, unknown, and available candidates over those that are known by the database but whose availability is not known to the recruiter, so external databases are often favored over internal, proprietary data.

- Recruiters may conduct sourcing activities outside of the firm's database, which means that some of the value-added data resides in the recruiter's personal network rather than the corporate ATS.

- Candidate talent pool development and management processes tend not to be well defined.

Key metrics

- Time and cost to fill

- Percent positions filled by source

- Yield ratio (e.g. screen, interview, submit and placement ratios)

- Candidate sourcing tools
- Corporate ATS
- Staffing front office
- Professional services automation (PSA) software
- Project/portfolio management software
- HRIS
- Corporate career site
- Candidate portal
- Employee portal
- Alumni portal
- VMS
- Job boards
- Referral, social, and professional networks
- Search and match technology
- Resume and contact parsing technology

Step 5: Assess and Select Talent

PROCESS OBJECTIVE

Efficiently hire the talent that is the best fit at the best price for a specific job requisition or project.

PROCESS OWNER

Head of recruitment

KEY STAKEHOLDERS

Business unit heads, hiring manager, head of HR

KEY ACTIVITIES

For job requisitions:

- Conduct skill tests and assessments.
- Schedule and conduct applicant interviews.
- Collect feedback and rank applicants.
- Assess any training needs (for internal candidates).
- Conduct background checks and drug screens (for external candidates).
- Check references.
- Negotiate offer.
- Get signed agreement.
- Capture compliance data (for external candidates).
- Update systems.

For statements of work:

- Receive notification of approved project.
- Review project requirements.
- Identify sources of HC (e.g. contractors, consultants, outsourcers).
- Manage RFx process and select finalists.
- Negotiation scope, price, and terms, and finalize statement of work.
- Get signed agreement.
- Update systems.

PROCESS INPUT

- Shortlisted candidates from "Step 4: Proactive and Reactive Skill Sourcing"
- Supplier rate cards
- All the tools necessary to rank candidates and make just-in-time decisions regarding the relative value of each worker type

PROCESS OUTPUT

- Filled requisitions and staffed projects
- Signed statements of work
- Compliance reports
- Training requirements for internally selected candidates (if needed)

Key process issues

- When it comes down to ranking qualified candidates, it is not always clear which resource or worker type is the most cost effective for the company.

- There can be a lot of inconsistency across recruiters around the screening and assessment process.

- Regulatory requirements make compliance reporting complex and often a lot of manual work is required.

- Because data is manually entered in most cases, data is often not entered into the system.

- The number of steps in this process is increasing, e.g. more forms, more background checks, more data entry and the status of the steps are often handled manually.

- E-signature is not widely adopted in HR and staffing, so there are a vast number of documents that must be signed and stored with the candidate record.

Key metrics

- Time to fill and cost to fill
- Percent positions filled by source
- Yield ratio (e.g. screen, interview, submit and placement ratios)
- Success ratio
- Percent turnover by position (expected versus actual)

Supporting Technology

- Candidate sourcing tools
- Corporate ATS
- Staffing front office
- PSA software
- Project/portfolio management software
- HRIS
- Corporate career site
- Candidate portal
- Employee portal
- Alumni portal
- VMS
- Search and match technology
- Technology enabled services for background checks, drug tests, skill tests, personality/behavioral assessments, and reference checking

Step 6: Onboard and Manage Talent and Projects

PROCESS OBJECTIVE

Ramp up talent so they are performing at or better than expectations as quickly as possible.

PROCESS OWNER

Head of HR

KEY STAKEHOLDERS

Business unit heads, hiring managers, head of recruitment

KEY ACTIVITIES

- Complete and manage new hire paperwork (e.g. I-9, W-4, confidentiality agreement).
- Obtain workspace, work equipment (e.g. PC, system logins, email, safety equipment, telephone) and physical security (e.g. security badge).
- Conduct orientation and coach new talent.
- Talent reports to worksite.
- Capture and approve time.
- Manage missing time.
- Manage attendance.
- Manage talent performance.
- Manage project performance.
- Manage compensation.
- Develop and train talent.

Process Input

- Ready-to-start talent
- Job descriptions
- Project plan, statement of work, and project management infrastructure

Process Output

- Approved timecards
- Oriented and training talent
- Performance reviews
- Project reviews and status reports

Key Process Issues

- Talent is either underutilized or overutilized.
- Onboarding process typically ends at orientation, resulting in suboptimal productivity and higher turnover, especially during the first year.
- Majority of companies still rely on manual paper timesheets.
- Hiring firms do not have visibility into liability associated with time until suppliers invoice them.
- Multiple, stand-alone systems used to support management of talent as well as projects and systems don't tie.
- High degree of variability exists across SOWs, so managing each project is unique.

Key metrics

- Turnover
- Time to productivity
- Hiring manager and talent satisfaction levels

Supporting technology

- Time and expense systems
- Time clocks
- Attendance tracking systems
- HRIS
- Project management software
- Document management systems
- Performance management systems
- Learning management and training delivery systems
- Identity management systems
- Asset management systems
- Security management systems
- Onboarding software
- Internal talent management systems

Step 7: Pay Talent and Suppliers

PROCESS OBJECTIVE

Provide accurate and timely payment for services rendered and be in compliance of all supplier contracts.

PROCESS OWNER

Accounting

KEY STAKEHOLDERS

CFO, suppliers, business unit heads, head of HR, head of procurement, hiring manager

KEY ACTIVITIES

For direct hires:

- Review approved hours, pay rate and pay rules (e.g. overtime).
- Manage missing time.
- Calculate pay, taxes, and deductions.
- Manage benefits eligibility, enrollment, and deductions.
- Manage garnishments.
- Process payroll.
- Calculate and approve recruiter bonus.
- Manage federal, state and local tax payments.
- Manage errors.

For indirect hires (supplier provided talent):

- Review approved hours, pay rate, and pay rules (e.g. overtime).
- Calculate gross amount due.
- Calculate sales tax and apply agreed discounts.
- Send electronic advice to supplier/VMS.

For suppliers (suppliers paying talent and invoicing clients):

- Review approved hours, pay rate, and pay rules (e.g. overtime) and verify for contact compliance.
- Calculate gross amount owed.
- Calculate sales tax and apply agreed discounts.
- Process invoice and submit to client.
- Receive electronic funds and apply cash to correct client, invoice and worker/project.
- Handle collections issues.
- Manage payment of supplier's sub-vendors.
- Same payroll processes as hiring companies (see above list for indirect hires).

PROCESS INPUT

- Approved time cards
- Agreed compensation and benefits
- Agreed payment terms, schedule, and method

PROCESS OUTPUT

- Paid talent
- Paid suppliers
- Deductions and tax liabilities managed

KEY PROCESS ISSUES

- Accounts payable for services may follow a different workflow for each worker type.
- Stakeholders have limited visibility into total labor spend because wages and benefits for direct staff typically are kept completely separate from dollars spent on the flexible workforce.
- Companies have been slow to adopt electronic time cards and payment methods.
- Companies continue to follow traditional A/R and A/P processes with paper invoicing from suppliers and have been slow to adopt self-bill approach.
- Complex rate cards, discounts, and terms make accurate supplier billing and contract compliance difficult to manage.

KEY METRICS

- Number of pay adjustments
- Number of live checks
- Number of billing errors (with suppliers)
- Number of late/early payments

Supporting Technology

- Time and expense management system
- HRIS
- Payroll processing provider
- Benefits management provider
- Tax update service
- Direct deposit and payment card
- Accounts payable software
- Back office and general ledger technology (for suppliers)

Step 8: Analyze Human Capital Spend and Results

PROCESS OBJECTIVES

- Achieve one-hundred-percent visibility into human capital spend across all divisions globally.
- Analyze actual workforce performance as compared to expectations.

PROCESS OWNER

Head of procurement

KEY STAKEHOLDERS

CEO, CFO, COO, business unit heads, head of HR, head of recruitment

KEY ACTIVITIES

- Capture and analyze human capital spend (estimated to actual) across all departments, labor types, geographies, etc.
- Identify any out-of-system spend or unexpected process variations.
- Compare and analyze optimal to actual talent mix.
- Compare and analyze workforce productivity and performance.
- Understand and measure hiring manager satisfaction levels.

- Evaluate and compare supplier performance and ensure contract compliance (e.g. pricing, yield ratios).
- Share supplier scorecards with supplier management.
- Audit rates and compensation to determine alignment with market and expectations.
- Document findings.
- Identify supply chain inefficiencies and opportunities to reduce spend and improve performance.
- Develop and execute improvement plans.

PROCESS INPUT

- Strategic workforce plan
- Talent acquisition plan
- Latest human capital spend analysis
- Agreed supplier scorecard template
- Human capital and supplier performance data

PROCESS OUTPUT

- Supplier scorecards
- Updated human capital spend analysis
- HCSC improvement initiatives (e.g. talent mix adjustments, technology improvements, supplier policy changes)

KEY PROCESS ISSUES

- Culture change for procurement as their focus has traditionally been on goods procurement not services or human capital procurement.
- Companies lack visibility into total human capital spend.
- Off-contract spend is rampant in most organizations.
- Spend and performance details are not easily available.
- Data available is disparate and inaccurate.

KEY METRICS

- Budget to actual spend
- Expected to actual performance
- Expected to actual talent mix
- Percent savings

SUPPORTING TECHNOLOGY

- Spend analysis software
- Satisfaction survey tools
- Supplier portal
- Data from all of the key systems including ATS, accounting, procurement, and VMS
- Reporting and business intelligence software

Health Check Your HCSCM Processes

Take the following quick wellness survey to rate how advanced your HCSCM processes are:

1	*We have a strategic workforce plan in place that addresses both our permanent and flexible workforce. We review our progress monthly and update the plan quarterly.*	*True*	*False*
2	*We have clearly stated goals which articulate how we would like to improve our HCSC within the next year.*	*True*	*False*
3	*We have total visibility into our global human capital costs across all worker types.*	*True*	*False*
4	*HR, procurement, finance, and business unit heads work in concert and follow a defined HCSCM process.*	*True*	*False*
5	*Everyone in the HCSC knows that they are responsible for improving its performance and eliminating costs.*	*True*	*False*
6	*New talent is brought on just in time; that is, they start on the desired date.*	*True*	*False*
7	*We continually work with our strategic suppliers to take cost out of the supply chain while increasing the quality of talent.*	*True*	*False*

8	*Our suppliers are informed of our talent acquisition plan and have access to an up-to-date and accurate performance dashboard.*	*True*	*False*
9	*One hundred percent of our timesheets are entered and approved online and there are virtually no payroll errors.*	*True*	*False*
10	*Our accounts payable process is streamlined and one hundred percent of our supplier payments are paid electronically. We track the liability continuously and have no need to receive supplier invoices.*	*True*	*False*

Total the number of questions you answered "True."

If you scored between:

0 and 3   You are falling behind the competition; get to work!

4 and 7   Good work, but your HCSC is nothing to brag about. There are still many improvements to make.

7 and 10   Impressive! You have robust HCSCM processes. Keep up the hard work and crush your competition.

- Designing a HCSCM process is fundamental to business and it's important to get your existing HCSC under control.

- There are eight key steps in the holistic HCSCM process that can be tailored to a specific situation and strategy. Document the process!

- Once an HCSCM process is in place, routinely analyze the performance and find ways to continually improve efficiency and cut costs.

- Emerging HCSCM processes are seamless, C-level led, strategic, continually measured, regularly tuned and fully automated.

- Hiring companies must look at total cost across the end-to-end supply chain and not push costs from one process to another (e.g. even if you push cost to suppliers, you are still paying for it).

- Focus on developing deep relationships with a handful of suppliers, especially those suppliers that are relentless about driving cost out of the supply chain while increasing the quality of talent.

Chapter 7: Tie the Technology Together

CHAPTER OBJECTIVES:

- Explain why automation across the HCSC is critical for business recovery and future growth.

- Describe the ultimate end-to-end, integrated HCSC software solution and its benefits.

- Identify the key software applications in the supply chain and how they are connected.

- Highlight the biggest inefficiencies in HCSC technology.

WINNING THE TALENT GRAB REQUIRES HCSC AUTOMATION

Economic recovery sparks fierce competition for top talent. The mad dash for top talent is won by firms that snatch up top talent the fastest. Growth and revenue is maximized by how quickly firms are able to hire and onboard human capital.

Strategic organizations position themselves to "flip the switch" and turn on their recruiting machine at the first opportunity. When the economy begins to turn around, firms that mobilize their rehiring and recruitment fastest with new HCSC methods are most successful in acquiring top talent. Organizations dependent on rehiring and ramping up their old recruiting functions are unlikely to win the race. Progressive organizations do not plan to come out of a recession in the traditional way; that is, they do not scale their recruiting function with masses of recruiters. Leading organizations put the necessary technology in place and enable their recruitment to scale through automation. Companies that are able to hire the best talent during the economic recovery are best positioned to accelerate their growth.

From a technology perspective, the best-positioned enterprises have a well-oiled and automated workforce planning, hiring, and onboarding capability that connects in real time to their talent suppliers, who are also fully automated and integrated. So, no matter what your role in the human capital supply chain, automation and integration are critical to success.

THE ULTIMATE, END-TO-END INTEGRATED HCSC

The diagram, below, illustrates the high-level technology components of the HCSC. The light-gray boxes represent the typical technology within a large organization. The dark-gray boxes represent technology provided by talent suppliers and other third-party service providers (e.g. background checking vendors). The arrows indicate high-level connections between systems.

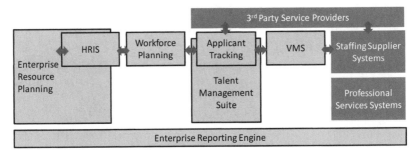

Figure 7: Typical Chain of HCSC Technology

The diagram shows the following chain of technology connections: enterprise resource planning (ERP) software (including procurement, financial management, and HRIS modules) to workforce planning software to applicant tracking (in order to accomplish all types of talent acquisition) to the VMS and on to the suppliers suite of systems. The web of software components and the two-way continuous flow of people-related information vary across organizations and are especially dependent upon the firm's size and talent needs.

The vendor management system has been shaded as if it is owned by the hiring organization, because its purpose is to serve the hiring company's needs and interests. The VMS may actually be supplied by a staffing vendor or a third party and be supplier-funded, but the key data within the VMS is owned by the hiring organization. The VMS plays a central and critical role in the HCSC because it is the technology that connects the hiring company to its talent suppliers. Ideally, all worker types are processed via the VMS so that the corporation finally has a complete view of all of its non-permanent workforce costs.

Human capital-related data must be readily available and driven by real-time customer and operational needs. While each system will likely have its own reporting capability, an overarching reporting and business intelligence capability is desired. The ability to combine data from each system enables an up-to-date view of performance across the entire human capital supply chain.

Hiring organizations are dependent on a chain of talent suppliers, including staffing firms, professional services organizations, executive search firms, and outsourcing organizations. From a technology perspective, all of the information relating to workforce planning and demand needs to be shared as quickly as possible with all suppliers. Real-time communication and just-in-time coordination with staffing suppliers around workforce needs enables the enterprise to minimize the time required to fill open positions.

Integrating your HCSC applications will yield massive benefits, including decreased time and cost to fill positions. While automated data exchange exists in pockets, it is not yet prevalent across the entire supply chain. Administrative costs are much higher when there is no automated data exchange between the third-party vendors and the HCSC. Additional administrative costs include duplicate data entry, researching and fixing downstream issues caused by data entry errors, reconciliation of data across multiple systems, as well as manual monitoring of adjacent systems, suppliers and third-party services.

TYPICAL INEFFICIENCIES IN HCSC TECHNOLOGY

There is much inefficiency in HCSC technology. Most weaknesses can be tied back to the fact that most firms have not formalized their HCSC and do not have a single owner of the end-to-end vision, process, or technology.

No single IT owner

Each system in the HCSC (see Figure 7) may be owned by a different department within the organization. Establishing an overarching owner of HCSC technology provides the opportunity to develop a longer-term vision and plan for implementing suitable technology and tying it together to maximize business performance.

Multiple systems of each type

Large corporations often have more than one system of each type. Larger organizations may find that they have purchased multiple applicant tracking systems, for example, to suit each country, business unit, skill group, or worker type. Clearly, having more systems makes the integration effort much more difficult. Disparate systems also make it nearly impossible to have a unified view of the workforce, not to mention the total cost of human capital.

Lack of automated data exchange between systems

There are a number of reasons why there is limited integration between HCSC systems, including lack of an end-to-end owner, too many systems of each type, the expense of integration, and the required cross-functional cooperation.

Lack of end-to-end terminology, standards, and data

As long as hiring companies use different terms and definitions for skills, competencies, metrics, and a variety of integration standards, the HCSC will not be able to operate at maximum efficiency levels.

THE TECHNOLOGY THAT TIES THE HCSC TOGETHER

This section describes the role of each HCSC technology from Figure 7 in greater detail.

ERP is not geared for HCSCM (yet)

Enterprise resource planning software has been evolving since the 1980s. ERP systems enable various departments and operating units including: accounting and finance, human resources, marketing, production, fulfillment, and distribution. ERP enables companies to coordinate activities, share information, and collaborate. ERP software ties together core business processes, including customer relationship management, supplier relationship management, order management, production and project planning, procurement, supply chain management, financial management, and human capital management (HCM).

While ERP vendors provide an end-to-end offering, their software is generally sold as individual components, which work together to automate the key business businesses. Figure 8 shows an example of how the ERP components might be offered and tied together to manage the corporation.

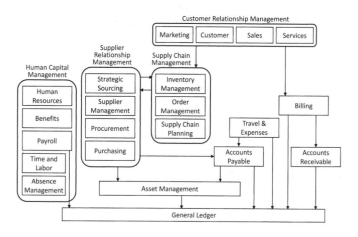

Figure 8: Sample Set of ERP Modules

ERP software was designed with a focus on business management and manufacturing, but has not yet succeeded in applying its manufacturing supply chain excellence to the procurement of human capital, even though human capital is the most important enabler of any enterprise. Examples of how ERP does not adequately address the needs of the HCSC include:

- Limited workforce planning functionality;

- Lack of a real-time feedback loop between production planning and workforce planning to tune workforce levels as well as limited linkages with your applicant tracking systems (ATS) and talent management suites (TMS);

- No linkages between the ERP, HRIS, and talent management system to maintain an up-to-date view of the permanent workforce;

- Unclear how non-permanent workforce time and costs are incorporated with permanent workforce costs to get a total view and cost of human capital; and

- No feed from workforce planning to an ATS and back to the supplier management module for automated staffing supplier management.

In manufacturing, production plan schedules are tied to business planning and tuned on nearly a real-time basis, whereas hiring plans are typically set on an annual basis and reviewed monthly. Data about the current levels of human capital are often pulled from several systems and reliant on manual tweaks. Changes in product demand tend to impact the hiring plan in a much-delayed manner, as evidenced by the mass layoffs in 2009. ERP systems, human capital management, and workforce planning processes must be tied together to get more accurate data about resource needs in a more efficient manner.

In addition to being driven by changes in production needs, workforce levels fluctuate on their own. Absence tracking and management on a day-to-day basis certainly drives workforce needs in a tactical way. On a more strategic level, voluntary employee turnover must also be accounted for in the workforce plan. Turnover can be measured and managed through retention and succession planning programs. This attendance, turnover, and succession-planning data must be tied together in order to get a more accurate picture of the current and expected workforce levels.

The HCSC demands an overall view of the workforce and ERP has not focused on providing a combined view of the permanent and flexible workforces. While all of the costs associated with labor may end up in the general ledger, labor-based expenses are often mixed with other non-labor costs and not properly categorized to provide a total cost of human capital and the supporting detail.

ERP typically focuses on the HCSC from a procurement perspective. ERP does its best to enable the effective procurement of any and all service categories, which is also known as services procurement. Services procurement includes a wide variety of business and labor-based services, such as contract labor, consultancy services, marketing, advertising, travel, telecommunications, financial and legal services. Procurement modules of ERP solutions were initially tailored towards procurement of materials and so ERP excels at providing functionality for centralized sourcing and contract management, automation of procure to pay, catalog management, supplier evaluation, and collaboration processes. Procurement of services in an organization is new territory and requires a unique skill set. Procurement organizations have been slow to leverage the ERP's services procurement functionality.

Organizations invest in ERP systems to reduce operating costs, improve operational visibility and implement tighter financial controls and compliance. Most ERP vendors provide industry-specific solutions such as banking, insurance, retail, manufacturing, health sciences, high-tech, and communications.

Although top-tier ERP solutions, Oracle (including PeopleSoft and JD Edwards) and SAP, provide end-to-end automation and are fully integrated out of the box, the implementation tends to be complex, costly, requires expensive IT specialists to configure, and is time-consuming to implement. Furthermore, major releases with new features and functionality are scheduled every two to three years and require clients to make additional investment to keep up with the upgrades.

While SAP and Oracle dominate the enterprise ERP market, Tier 2 vendors (e.g. Agresso, Epicor, Exact, Infor and Microsoft) provide similar functionality at a much lower cost to small, mid-size and niche businesses. Based on open, flexible, service-oriented architecture (SOA) with web-based user interfaces, Tier 2 ERP vendors offer lower cost of ownership, usage, and maintenance and provide multiple buying options, including SaaS. Most Tier 2 solutions are easy to use and fast to implement. Some of these vendors, such as Infor, provide separate ERP applications by industry; that is, they incorporate predefined business roles and business process specific to the industry to enable a swift implementation.

ERP plays a key role in the HCSC and the enterprise, but its functionality and capabilities aren't mature when it comes to HCSC automation. ERP needs to accelerate its enablement of the HCSC and, in the meantime, strategic firms need to drive their vendors to make it happen, define the end-to-end business process, and begin to stitch together the pieces.

Workforce Planning Software

There is an urgent need to capture real-time workforce demand data from various inputs and to determine workforce needs across the organization as well as on a location, position, and skill-by-skill basis. Just as critical is the understanding of the lead time to hire key skill sets and the various resource costs by worker type (e.g. permanent employee, temporary employee, contractor, consultant). Workforce planning software links people and production planning activities to the HCSC and enables organizations to trigger the hiring of the right people at exactly the right time.

Organizations have engaged in workforce planning throughout history. Even the designers of the pyramids had to figure out what kind of workforce they needed to get the job done. Workforce planning was known as "manpower" planning in the 1960s and later as "human resources" planning. The need for workforce planning has increased because of changing views of work, employees seeking to change organizations throughout their careers, new skills required for new technologies and changing demographics. Workforce planning, often an annual event, needs to be an ongoing and continuous activity in order to provide competitive advantage to the organization and minimize total human capital costs.

Workforce planning solutions aggregate and unify data from the HRIS, talent management systems, financial system, and other internal and external sources. Workforce planning is no longer limited to a pile of spreadsheets and statistics. These software applications help businesses identify the skill sets already available within the existing workforce along with skill gaps. Additionally, based on internal workforce trends and market assumptions, the solutions help project the workforce strength, skill requirements, and talent mix needed in the future.

Workforce planning vendors include: Aruspex, Infohrm, and Vemo.

Human Resource Information System (HRIS)

HRIS continues to have an important role within the organization as it is the system of record for all payroll- and benefits-related information. Typical HRIS functionality includes the employee data for all current and past employees, benefits eligibility and enrollment, timecard submissions and approvals, absence management, payroll preparation, and employee self-service. Employee payroll- and benefits-related data is generally passed along for payroll processing and benefits delivery, but may be handled by the HRIS as well. HRIS may also handle recruitment, simple tracking of training, certification, and performance reviews, but talent management suites offer more sophisticated functionality in each of these areas.

The HRIS was the centerpiece of HR software within the enterprise, prior to the wide adoption of TMS. HRIS evolution started with payroll systems, which matured over time and started holding more and more employee information. The HRIS market grew rapidly in the '80s and '90s. In the early- to mid-2000s, companies started to integrate separate HR functions into a fuller "hire to separation" process, which drove HRIS systems to broaden their functionality. While HRIS solutions are offered as separate software packages, a number of ERP and TMS vendors also include HRIS functionality. The terms human resource management system (HRMS) and human capital management software are often used interchangeably with HRIS, but it is generally understood that HRMS and HCM offer richer functionality, with HRMS tending toward a combined HRIS and TMS solution and HCM tending toward a more robust HRIS system.

HRIS vendors include: Ascentis, Bond, NuView, Sage, Sapien, and Ultimate.

Talent Management Suites (TMS)

Talent management suite software is used to manage the permanent workforce. TMS provides deep and integrated functionality for a variety of HR functions including performance, compensation, succession, learning, competencies, career planning, and recruitment. Most TMS applications integrate with HRIS systems. The TMS concept was born during the mid-2000s and the concept has centered in on the total management and development of direct employees.

The recruitment portion of the TMS provides critical functionality to the HCSC because it enables the organization to bring outside talent into the organization. The recruitment module is used to acquire outside talent directly through the company's recruiting team and indirectly, through staffing suppliers. The recruitment module is often referred to as the applicant tracking system or the talent acquisition system (TAS). The term recruitment management system (RMS) is also used at times. Because it is so critical to the HCSC, recruitment functionality is discussed more thoroughly later in this chapter.

The learning management and succession planning module plays a role in the HCSC since they provide the mechanisms to provide the key to identifying potential internal sources of talent.

TMS vendors tend to be strong in a single area (e.g. performance management) and build out their TMS from that base. Because TMS modules are quite feature-rich, TMS vendors spend a great deal of development or acquisition dollars expanding their suite. Because development dollars are spread thin, TMS vendors tend to slow their investment in their recruitment modules because they are already mature with rich sets of functionality. This practice frees up development budget for other, less-developed components of their suite. The TMS space is quite competitive where TMS buyers are looking for integrated suites, so TMS vendors must fill in any component gaps in order to remain competitive.

TMS vendors include: Authoria, Bond, HRSmart, SuccessFactors, Taleo, and Workday.

Applicant Tracking Systems (ATS)

Applicant tracking systems emerged in the '90s to automate the recruitment and hiring process. ATS functionality matured and became the core tool for talent acquisition in companies of all sizes. Applicant tracking systems facilitate requisition approval and management, applicant tracking, capture of online applications, job distribution, resume processing, screening and assessment, compliance and diversity management, and onboarding. Various screens, interviews, and checks such as phone screens, in-person interviews, skill tests, background checks, and reference checks may be required and are tracked in the ATS, even when third-party providers are used. In addition, the system stores the resume and profile data for all candidates including their education, certifications, and work history. ATS can parse candidate information directly into the system and offer sophisticated searching capabilities. ATS support EEOC and OFFCP tracking and reporting, job distribution to external job boards, candidate source tracking; and a few of them support multiple languages. ATS also enable organizations to automatically track recruitment metrics such as time to hire, candidates per source, hires per source, average time open, and more. ATS include corporate career sites and candidate portals that facilitate the completion of employment applications and preliminary screening (e.g. knock-out questions) online.

ATS grew to enable internal mobility for internal employees and alumni-management solutions. A number of systems offer candidate relationship management functionality that enables the development of candidate communities that may serve as sources for future openings. Some vendors integrated their products with Web 2.0 technologies and social networking sites such as LinkedIn, Facebook, and Twitter to enable organizations to leverage social networks for recruiting purposes.

Applicant tracking systems automate and simplify the recruitment process, enable collaboration between recruiter and hiring manager, improve the candidate's experience, and provide end-to-end recruitment workflows, i.e. from hiring to onboarding. The core benefit of an ATS is in its ability to reduce the cost and time to fill a position.

The level of functionality, service, and cost varies greatly across ATS providers. Most ATS vendors provide their clients the option to customize the application to suit their requirements. The extent to which the application is configurable varies from vendor to vendor.

ATS vendors commonly price their products based on number of users (employees and/or recruiters), number of hires and other factors. Mr. Ted was one of the few to introduce a free ATS, called SmartRecruiters. The solution is free to companies with fewer than 2,500 employees.

ATS vendors include: ADP, Bernard Hodes, Bond, Ceridian, First Advantage, iCIMS, Kenexa, Mr. Ted, Peopleclick, SilkRoad, SmartSearch, and Taleo.

Vendor Management Systems (VMS)

Vendor management systems enable hiring companies to electronically distribute job orders to multiple staffing suppliers for fulfillment. VMS have a pivotal role in the HCSC in that they connect the corporation to their staffing suppliers and provide greater visibility into a company's spend on labor.

The development of vendor management systems came about in the '90s. The great attraction to hiring companies is that VMS automates all key aspects of the procurement of temporary, contract, contract-to-hire, permanent, and project-based workers from a wide variety of staffing suppliers. Before the Internet, it was nearly impossible to create a competitive environment for an individual job requisition, especially in the temporary market when the average time to fill is typically measured in hours, not days. Hiring managers didn't have enough time to evaluate faxed résumés from multiple suppliers in the timeframe required. The VMS web-based interface finally provided that mechanism. Hiring companies wanted the ability to create private marketplaces where they could pick the suppliers they wished to compete for a specific requisition. Most large enterprises have a hundred (if not hundreds) of human capital suppliers that can be managed using VMS software and tiered, where different categories of suppliers receive a new order at different time intervals.

VMS software usually includes supplier tier management, order entry and fulfillment, candidate submittal and assignment, candidate time capture and approval, invoicing, payment, and reporting functionality. VMS have web-based user interfaces so they can be remotely accessed by the organization managing the VMS program as well as all approved suppliers and hiring managers for the review of submitted candidates and time card approval. The human capital procurement process for every VMS customer is highly unique and complex. Leading VMS software firms have invested substantially in making their software highly configurable via administrative panels so that they can get new enterprise customers up and running quickly on a software-as-a-service (SaaS) architecture.

Consolidated staffing supplier spend reporting is the strongest justification for the use of VMS software. Large enterprise customers often lack visibility into their spending on services, and utilize VMS reports to build a picture of their contingent labor and consulting expenditures. In addition, VMS implementations typically reduce labor costs by five to twenty percent in the year they are implemented.

VMS is a technology solution that must be managed by a program office. In the majority of cases, the VMS is managed directly by the corporation. There is a growing trend for companies to outsource VMS management to managed service providers. In their purest form, MSPs are completely vendor neutral and do not fill any of the firm's positions themselves. In other cases, a corporation might hire a master vendor (MV) to manage their contingent labor program. The MSP and MV may provide VMS technology packaged with their program office services. In any case, the VMS is almost always supplier funded, meaning the supplier pays the program office and VMS vendor a percentage (approximately one to three percent) of the total dollars managed by the system.

VMS vendors include: Beeline, Bond, Fieldglass, IQNavigator, Peopleclick, ProcureStaff, PrO Unlimited, Provade, TAPFIN, and WorkforceLogic.

Enterprise Reporting and Business Intelligence

Reporting and business intelligence have all become more affordable and pervasive. Individual software applications across the HCSC typically include good reporting functionality and varying levels of analysis and business intelligence capability.

While system-specific reports are helpful, a consistent view of the current status across the entire HCSC is mandatory.

Real-time visibility into customer orders, production level changes, workforce needs, and labor costs for all worker types is required. Customized, role-based dashboards that present HCSC-wide performance data can enable stakeholders to maximize HCSC efficiency.

Enterprise reporting and business intelligence vendors include: Business Objects (SAP), Cognos (IBM), Hyperion (Oracle), Information Builders, Microsoft, and Microstrategy.

Staffing Supplier Systems

Every corporation uses staffing suppliers to fill a number of permanent, contract, and temporary positions. Companies tend to have anywhere between a handful and a hundred key staffing suppliers. Time to fill is typically critical, so the entire network of staffing suppliers must be linked to the HCSC.

Staffing front office systems have most of the functionality offered by applicant tracking systems and then some. First of all, staffing systems must manage a complex customer hierarchy, a number of client contacts, contracts, and customer-specific workflows and requirements as well as sales pipeline tracking and management. Front office systems may also include client portals and limited vendor management functionality. Staffing front office systems must support pay and bill rates for each assignment and capture enough information about the assignment to hand-off to back office accounting systems for weekly (or even daily) billing and payroll.

Another key difference between software that supports a staffing firm, and those that are corporate HR focused, is that a staffing firm expects to staff candidates on multiple, successive assignments. Since staffing firms tend to deal with much higher volumes of candidates, there is more complexity around tracking key documents such as consent forms, I-9s, W-4s, and client-specific forms.

Staffing firms must capture candidate time, which is then used to pay candidates and bill clients. While corporate systems also capture employee time and process employee payroll, back office staffing systems must also bill clients. When a VMS is involved, no bill is sent from the staffing firm. Rather, the staffing firm compares their internally generated bill with that of the VMS. The VMS pays the staffing firm based on approved hours and rates in the VMS. The hiring company makes a single consolidated payment to the VMS for all hours worked by all staffing suppliers. When a VMS is not in the picture, the staffing supplier sends their invoice to the hiring manager or the client's accounts payable department and waits for payment. An interesting challenge for most staffing firms is that they must use credit line funding to pay their weekly payrolls until they receive their customer's payment thirty to sixty days later. It is increasingly common for hiring companies to automatically pay staffing suppliers based on the approved time in the client's internal time capture system. This "invoice-less" approach saves everyone in the supply chain a great deal of time and money because it is so efficient.

Staffing software vendors include: Bond, Bullhorn, Maxhire, Oracle/PeopleSoft, PAM, Sage, Sendouts, SmartSearch, VCG, and TempWorks.

Professional Services Systems

Professional services firms typically capture their order as a statement of work. While SOWs are increasingly being routed through a VMS, they are more typically monitored and tracked outside of any centrally managed program. Most firms do not have a handle on how much money is actually being spent on consulting services across their organization. Without visibility into their total spend on consulting services, CFOs and procurement teams are unable to ensure consistent bill rates, negotiate preferred pricing, or track contract compliance.

The consulting firm most likely enters the SOW and assigns resources in their internal professional services automation system. There are a variety of payment approaches outlined in the SOW, including time and materials, milestone or deliverable based, not to exceed or fixed project amounts. The PSA tool or downstream software generates bills that are sent to the client's engagement manager or directly to accounts payable. Since the PSA tool is not integrated with the VMS, the professional services firm and the hiring company will need to reconcile the professional services firm's invoice with the VMS invoice. This reconciliation process and the resulting clean-up and correction work can be quite time consuming.

PSA software vendors include: NetSuite, OpenAir, Oracle/ PeopleSoft, and QuickArrow.

Technology-Enabled Third-party Services

Third-party services are a growing component of the HCSC. There are a variety of software-based services that are used along the human capital supply chain, including:

- Job boards (e.g. CareerBuilder, Monster)
- Job board distributors (e.g. Broadbean, Data Frenzy, eQuest, Job VIPeR, SmartPost)
- Online recruiter exchanges (e.g. BountyJobs, Dayak, public and private splits organizations)
- Contractor networks (e.g. Elance, HotGigs, Sologig.com)

- Candidate sourcing tools and sites (e.g. AIRS, Data Frenzy, InfoGIST, TalentDrive, TalentHook)

- Background check and drug test providers (e.g. ADP, Lexis Nexus, Choicepoint, First Advantage, Intelius, Quest Diagnostics, Sterling Testing)

- Skills assessments providers (e.g. Brainbench, Prove It!, SkillCheck)

- Personality and other non-skill assessments (e.g. ePredix, PeopleAnswers, PreVisor)

- Payroll service providers (e.g. ADP, Ascentis, Ceridian, Paychex)

- Benefits administration (e.g. Aflac, BlueCross, Unum)

- Tax update services (e.g. Greenshades, Symmetry, Vertex)

As you can see, there are a diverse set of vendors that add value to the overall hiring process. These vendors exchange data with the core set of HCSC systems.

Manual, duplicate data entry between the third party and the supply chain is commonplace and can severely slow down processes. For example, a recruiter might be holding up an offer while they try to find time to log into their background checker's online portal to see if a result has been posted. This manual status checking adds a great deal of additional administrative time or cost to the requisition and also lengthens the time to fill, without adding any value to the process.

Additionally, many technology-enabled services can be considered commodity services (e.g. background checking), so the ability to quickly switch to the lowest-cost provider without having to retrain recruiters would provide great cost savings.

SPEAKING A COMMON LANGUAGE

Key data that links the supply chain

There are a few major entities moving up and down the human capital supply chain that are used to communicate needs and procure talent.

Job Requisitions/Order. Job requisitions (the term used by corporations) or job orders (the term used by staffing firms) communicate the resource need. Articulating a need for human capital is not as easy as placing an order for office supplies. Each job requisition represents a ranked and weighted set of requirements. Each candidate may have a different combination of skills and experience and may not fit the exact job requirements. Until the job is filled, there is an ongoing and dynamic fuzzy matching between the requirements in the requisition and the quality of available talent, which makes the requisition specifications somewhat murky.

In many cases the requisition does not include enough data to fill the position. When job requisitions are handed off to suppliers for fulfillment there are two schools of thought on what should happen next. The majority of staffing firms want to pick up the phone to find out more about the order and tend not to document their findings in the system. The other set of staffing suppliers believes they should know the client well enough to know what talent is needed and should be able to get to work on filling the order. The latter case is clearly more efficient that the former.

Skills and competencies. Skill names and definitions vary widely across organizations in the supply chain, which makes it difficult to quickly interpret the needs of the job requisition and the fit of each candidate. This is much easier in the manufacturing ERP system where a part number denotes a specific set of characteristics across all suppliers. Each customer and staffing supplier has a different set of skills that they use to index their candidates. Using different skill and competency terms and models makes it difficult to efficiently map skills lists in the job description to the candidate skills coded in any single database along the supply chain. Without a shared dictionary of skills and competencies, each organization in the chain loses efficiency as they must first map the client's skill needs to their own internal language. Skill sets of suitable candidates must be mapped back to the client's lingo before they are presented. While there are some examples of shared competency models (e.g. reusable definition of competency or educational objective (RDCEO), there is no prevalent competency model across the HR industry.

Time. The function and accuracy of time varies across the supply chain. Time is critical because it results in money and candidates flowing through the supply chain. The requisition starts off with an estimated length of assignment. Candidate availability must be determined relative to timing of the assignment. Part-time, project, and shift work can make assessing availability quite complex. Once the assignment is made, the worker submits his or her time, which may be assessed based on union, company-specific, local, state, or federal employment rules. Time approval can become complicated with multiple approvers being fairly common. Companies must also accommodate state rules on whether time must be paid, whether or not it is approved. In short, accurate time collection and processing is highly complex and also the financial driver behind the HCSC.

Adding even further complexity, time flows into the supply chain in a number of places (e.g. paper timesheets, client system, VMS, staffing supplier system) and this causes inefficiencies when there are discrepancies, which there often are.

HR-XML Interoperability Standards

The HR-XML (an Extensible Markup Language specific to HR) was founded in 1999 as an independent, non-profit organization dedicated to the development and promotion of a standard suite of XML specifications to enable e-business and the automation of human resources-related data exchanges between hiring companies, vendors, and staffing suppliers. With more than 120 member organizations around the world, HR-XML is one of the largest and best-supported groups developing XML standards in support of specific business functions and is the recognized standards body for the HR industry. HR-XML schemas are often used to facilitate data exchange across the HCSC. While there are a number of strong HR-XML supporters, some vendors have defined their own integration standards. In most cases, these vendor proprietary standards are based loosely on HR-XML.

KEY POINTS: TIE THE TECHNOLOGY TOGETHER

- Companies that automate and integrate their end-to-end HCSC will be best positioned to accelerate their growth, especially as the economy recovers from a recession.

- Key technology in the HCSC includes: ERP, HRIS, workforce planning software, ATS, VMS, and the suite of staffing supplier software.

- VMS is critical and central to the HCSC because it is the link between the firm and the staffing suppliers. Most importantly, VMS has the potential to provide a complete view of spending on non-permanent workers.

- Integrating the technology across the HCSC will reduce the time and cost of filling positions by eliminating duplicate data entry and its associated errors, substantially reducing manual reconciliation of data between systems and time wasted manually bridging workflows and hand-offs between systems.

- Each of the systems in the supply chain is highly sophisticated and feature-rich. Many companies implement ERP in order to reduce the integration effort that is required with a best-of-breed approach.

Chapter 8: Create a Strategic Workforce Plan

CHAPTER OBJECTIVES:

- Explain the basics of what goes into an effective strategic workforce plan.

- Explain why workforce plans need to be closely tied to corporate strategy and how they drive the HCSC.

- Learn how to strategically expand your supply of human capital.

WHAT IS STRATEGIC WORKFORCE PLANNING?

Corporations clearly need to understand how human capital enables their business strategies and goals. A strategic workforce plan analyzes human capital demand and supply from the corporation's point of view. No matter what the industry, human capital plays a key role in the ability to deliver products and services. At the same time, the total cost of the workforce must be tightly managed as it represents such a major proportion of the operating expenses. Acquiring and retaining the best qualified, best fit, highest-performing talent for the best price is paramount for any organization. The plan must consider the total workforce, which includes both permanent staff and the flexible workforce (e.g. contractors, consultants, temps). Strategic workforce planning is the data-driven approach to determining exactly which skills a company needs at any given time in the future, the location where the talent is needed and the most cost-effective resource type (e.g. full-time, temp, contractor, consultant). Strategic workforce planning is essential to HCSC management and provides the rationale and the data, justifying the workforce size and cost. The strategic workforce plan is not a one-time strategy, rather it is a working plan that needs to be reviewed and updated routinely. The strategic workforce planning system must be tightly integrated with operational and financial systems so that weekly human capital demand fluctuations can be proactively detected and the appropriate action taken.

Strategic workforce planning has evolved more rapidly in recent years. New methodology and tools have been developed to help streamline and automate the typically manual process. Industry organizations and working groups have sprouted up and have significantly advanced the discipline.

Workforce plans are unique to each specific organization and differ based on a variety of factors, including the company's differentiators, company culture, the availability of skill sets and the corporate goals. For example, a company that differentiates on service considers their talent's ability to deliver that high-end service as key and retention will be a priority. A company that relies on unskilled labor, like much of the retail industry, is more likely to view talent as replaceable and their workforce plan will reflect the need to anticipate turnover and acquire low-cost talent quickly. Their workforce plan will support volume acquisition. A company with a strong culture will need to grow talent internally and carefully manage the acquisition of outside hires.

Why is Workforce Forecasting so Hard?

There are several drivers that make human capital planning so difficult:

Culture change for HR. Strategic workforce planning requires deep data-analysis skills. Human resources has been striving to develop their analytical skill sets. Much progress has been made to develop the science of HR, but a massive shift in the culture of HR as well as the retraining of HR professionals is required and that doesn't happen overnight.

New discipline. Most companies have limited data sets and limited knowledge about workforce planning. Being data-driven requires having the analytical skills, tools, processes, and systems in place. While some form of workforce planning has always been around, the discipline of strategic workforce planning is still evolving.

Dynamic markets. Our companies, our competitive markets, our economy, and our world seem to be shifting and changing continuously and dramatically. Workforce forecasting in such a dynamic environment is complex.

It's hard to be wrong. Forecasts are, by definition, just a best guess about what is going to happen. It's not easy to work with poor historical data, look forward to an uncertain future, and develop a workforce plan, knowing that even your best, most-educated guesses will be off.

What is Included in a Strategic Workforce Plan?

Strategic workforce plans look into the future as far as possible, which is typically one to three years. Because our world is increasingly dynamic, strategic plans have great detail in the near-term (i.e. next year or two) and are less defined after that. While plans may be less definite over longer time periods, corporations can still have a strategic outlook and more qualitative goals that address long-term supply and demand changes.

One of the key characteristics of a strategic workforce plan is that it is data-driven and constantly updated. While commercial workforce planning software has become available in the past few years, the majority of strategic workforce planners import data from the HRIS system into Microsoft Excel for analysis and running what-if scenarios.

The strategic workforce plan must address both the permanent and flexible workforce. That is, the strategic workforce plan must describe the desired workforce holistically and in its entirety.

Today, the permanent workforce is often planned separately from the flexible workforce and without consideration of the full picture of labor that is required to streamline the corporation.

Strategic workforce plans typically include the following six key sections:

1. **Current staffing levels and situation.** This portion of the strategic workforce plan describes current staffing levels and total human capital spend, broken down by category.

   Demographics of the current workforce are important to help detect potential issues such as baby boomer retirements. The current flow of talent, both from the supply and demand perspectives, should also be described.

2. **Corporate goals and market assumptions.** The plan must describe the role of human capital in enabling corporate strategies and goals. Key human capital strategies, such as the view on internal mobility, must also be articulated.

   Forces impacting talent supply and demand over time should be described and it is worth recapping current supply and demand issues. All of the potential forces that could impact talent supply and demand must be considered (e.g. local market, industry specific, macroeconomic). Both internal and external factors must be brainstormed.

   What-if scenarios are run to assess the impacts of each internal and external supply and demand change, so that the actual skill shortfall or surplus will be well understood and effectively sized.

3. **Future staffing levels.** The total human capital need and cost must be estimated over time (including timing of skills and needs by geography), with a focus on the next few years. Assumptions and confidence levels behind estimated numbers must be documented.

4. **Skill shortages, surpluses, and solutions.** Skill shortfalls and surpluses must be articulated, sized, and prioritized. The skill gap prioritization criteria must be noted for future reference.

   Both internal and external talent as well as a full suite of worker types must be considered for filling the talent gaps. Length of need, importance of position, time to fill, cost per hire, etc., must all be analyzed on a gap-by-gap basis.

   Short- and long-term action plans to resolve anticipated skill shortages and surpluses must be developed for each geographic region and division. The data developed in this section of the workforce plan is especially relevant to the process of talent acquisition planning.

5. **Optimal talent mix.** Based on the skill shortage and surplus solution analysis, goals around the mix of talent are determined.

6. **Strategic plan measurement and maintenance.** The document must also explain how the effectiveness of the strategic plan will be measured and reported.

The plan is meant to be a working document, so it is critical to identify how often the plan will be updated and reviewed and who is responsible for accomplishing this task. It is wise to identify key business triggers and early warning indicators that will result in an immediate review of the plan.

MAJOR SHIFTS IN DEMAND

The objective of workforce demand forecasting is to anticipate all future human capital needs of the corporation, across business units, product lines, geographies, and skill sets. There are many business and economic changes that drive major shifts in human capital demand:

Geographic expansion

Expanding operations into new territories requires addressing the need for talent in new and different locations. When geographic expansion is really global expansion, there is likely to be a great deal of knowledge to be integrated and understood around employment law and regulation, hiring practices, employee rights, etc., which feeds into the strategic plan and workforce decisions.

New products

The introduction of new products or product lines often requires new skill sets. Depending on whether the product replaces or extends existing offerings makes a difference in terms of skill gaps. Timing of product development, launch dates, and ongoing production must all be considered in the strategic plan.

Major changes in demand for your product or service

Fluctuations in client or consumer demand for the products or services have a major impact on the strategic workforce plan. The stage of the product in its life cycle and the growth projections will drive the roles and number of people required to support the product.

Economic shifts

Macroeconomic trends drive overarching client and consumer demand, which can massively impact revenue forecasts and associated workforce plans. As we've seen during recessions, these economic shifts can affect businesses across all product lines and geographies.

UNDERSTANDING THE SUPPLY OF TALENT

The objective of workforce supply forecasting is to understand all of the potential sources of human capital that could service as pipelines of skills and talent to the organization. The key is to understand the relative cost and benefit of each source and worker type so that the correct mix of resource types, that is, the mix with the greatest value-add, will be brought into the organization just in time.

The Internal Labor Pool

The internal labor pool is the most accessible and best-known talent pool. Just understanding the skills, capabilities, and preferences of the existing workforce can be a major undertaking on its own. Large organizations have a great deal of information about their workforce in their HRIS systems, but it does not typically include the skill information needed to effectively source talent internally.

There has been a push to consider internal talent for open positions before looking outside for new talent. This shift to enable, and perhaps even facilitate, internal mobility has resulted in the need to track and update employee skills routinely. Many corporations have started to keep these types of employee profiles separated from external labor pools so they can better leverage their internal workforce. Companies use a variety of tools, which may include: custom systems, ATS that support internal mobility, intranets, and enterprise professional networking solutions. Unfortunately, most corporations do not have these internal skill systems in place for their existing employees.

The internal talent pool may be considered strategic and a highly valued source of human capital or it may not. The value placed on the current workforce varies by organization. Companies that have invested in acquiring their workforce or those that have a strong culture, are most likely to fill positions with internal resources first. On the other hand, companies that expect or benefit from high turnover, like retail, may only look to their internal candidate pool for key positions.

Corporations have traditionally had little insight into their internal talent pool. Having basic profile data is a good first step, but being able to factor in more employee career goals and complex situations (e.g. part-time workers and virtual workforces) will result in higher retention rates and higher employee satisfaction at a lower cost of human capital. It is critical that a company's HRIS or TMS system includes an embedded skill-matching capability to fill new openings from the internal labor pool before exploring external labor pools.

In the early '90s, a new hiring manager at IBM was looking for a very unique circuit designer. The hiring manager engaged an expensive headhunter to locate this very unique person, and a few days later the headhunter called the hiring manager back with some good news. The headhunter had located the ideal candidate, who sat only eight offices down the hall from the hiring manager.

At Control Data Computers in the 1980s, it was not uncommon for managers to block their best employees from hearing about and applying for new job opportunities in different divisions of this 45,000-person company.

These two stories reinforce the need to have internal skill-matching systems where all employees can apply for positions that their skills qualify them for, and skill-matching systems where hiring managers can also search for qualified internal candidates. If a company does not have such an internal system, this should be added to the HCSC action plan.

External Labor Pools

There are a vast number of labor pools external to the organization. Once the decision to go outside for human capital has been made, companies need to strategically identify their preferred sourcing options. The default hiring choice has tended to be permanent, full-time staff and then fall back on contingent labor if the time to fill is too long for direct hires. This approach is outdated, overly simplistic, and frequently the least cost-effective approach. Corporations need to understand the trade-offs across their labor options relative to the total cost of human capital, productivity, duration of need, employment preference of the needed skill set, and then analytically determine the sourcing approach for each skill gap.

Clearly, the direct, full-time model has been the outdated default approach for filling open positions, but it is often not the most cost-effective approach for the organization. Companies must be more sophisticated and have a variety of employment relationships with their workforce in order to maximize profit and manage the cost of human capital. There are different costs and benefits to the organization for each type of employment relationship.

Temps and contractors. Temporary workforces are the best hedge against uncertain future demand. Temporary labor supplied by staffing companies provides short-term human capital to fill short-term needs. Temporary labor generally augments the existing workforce and is typically paid on an hourly basis.

Contractors are another form of contingent labor that may be used. Fuzzy co-employment rules around contractors increase the business risk of this resource type. We know that relatively scarce skill sets often prefer independent contractor status, e.g. software engineers, making this category a less ideal, but sometimes necessary choice. In some cases, contractors will take on business status directly or via third-party firms to reduce risk.

The downside of temps and contract labor is that there is no long-term commitment on either side. So, these short-term workers tend not to be treated as part of the organization and, as would be expected, their motivations are not tightly aligned with the corporation. If temporary workers end up staying for longer than expected, a direct resource may have been cheaper after all and there may be additional co-employment risk.

The upside of temporary and contract labor is that it is easy and inexpensive to ramp down or ramp up this flexible workforce. Analysts argue that there is always some level of demand uncertainty and companies should consistently maintain contingent labor levels of fifteen to twenty percent in order to mitigate market unknowns.

Consultants. While temporary and contractor labor is often paid by the hour, consulting firms are generally paid by the project. While consultants may have an hourly rate, they are typically responsible for a pre-defined set of deliverables and specific project outcomes. Consultants are most typically hired as a team and provide more senior, specialized human-capital-based services. They are expected to provide their own project oversight and manage team resources.

Relationships with professional services firms are often established at high levels within the organization and this is another reason that consulting firms are considered different from temporary and contractor arrangements. However, consulting projects increasingly fall under mainstream procurement, workforce planning, and management processes.

The downside of using consultants is that they tend to have much higher hourly rates than temporary or contract labor because they offer a highly specialized knowledge base and come as a skilled team. The overall cost for consultants can be much higher if the actual skill demanded is needed for a long period of time.

The upside of consultants is that they can provide high value-add to the organization very quickly because they are leveraging their past experience and offer skilled resources.

Outsourcers. Companies may decide to hand over non-core business functions to business process outsourcing companies. While consultants are responsible for delivering on project goals, BPOs are charged with delivering both business performance and business outcomes. There has been a trend for companies of all sizes to outsource a variety of functions including human resources, recruitment, accounting, manufacturing, distribution, and more.

In some cases, current employees are handed over to the BPO and become their employees. In many others cases, the outsourcer is offshore and the demand for specific skills shift offshore, especially to India, China, or Russia.

BPO decisions are highly strategic and longer term; they can be an effective way of cutting costs and increasing the profitability of a company, so outsourcing is likely to be part of a corporation's talent mix.

Direct or permanent hires. Direct hires can be the most cost-effective option when there is a long-term need for the skill or when a high degree of alignment with corporate goals and values is required. As we have stated, there has traditionally been a preference for full-time direct hires in every case, but now more attention must be paid to the most cost-effective, highest value-add worker type.

STRATEGICALLY EXPANDING THE SUPPLY OF TALENT

Every company should be continually expanding the supply of needed skill sets. There are a number of short- and long-term approaches for actively increasing access to the total supply of human capital available to the organization. Knowing who future employees might be is not enough; the firm must strive to have a stronger relationship with relevant talent than their competitors so that the talent is aware of the employment value and, when the timing is right, the best possible talent can be hired just in time. Here are eight ways to strategically expand human capital supply:

1. **Communicate long-term skill set needs to suppliers routinely.** Communicate skill needs to strategic suppliers so that they can proactively source needed skill sets over the long term on your behalf.

2. **Automate talent pipelining.** Once potential talent is identified, use technology to remain in continual contact to develop and deepen that relationship with talent over time. That way, you are in the best position to hire when you are in need of that skill set and the talent is ready to make a move.

3. **Offer professional development opportunities to internal talent.** Offer training, retraining, tuition assistance, leadership programs, or bonuses for certifications to the current workforce. This approach will help motivate the existing talent pool to continually develop their skills. Provide existing talent access to job openings and conduct succession planning for all key positions to help increase workforce engagement.

4. **Improve your candidate experience.** Improve the candidate's experience in order to attract the best talent.

5. **Improve your employee experience.** Improve the employee's experience in order to retain the best talent.

6. **Reach out and involve the community.** Develop community and educational outreach programs to increase the availability of key skill sets over the long term. Publicize expected skill needs to industry and trade associations. Conduct press campaigns to get the word out, so that the community as well as local universities and technical colleges can offer the necessary education to fill your needs over the long term. Support diversity efforts in order to remove some of the barriers to entry for ethnic and minority groups.

7. **Lobby for immigration and regulatory changes.** Lobby government in order to increase your ability to access skilled workers, and workforces regardless of where they live. Lobby for legislation that reduces the total cost of human capital.

8. **Source talent on a global basis.** Gain access to the worldwide set of relevant human capital through the use of global job boards, such as Monster or CareerBuilder, as well as the use of global staffing and professional services firms, such as Manpower, Adecco, Kelly Services, IBM, and Accenture.

ROUTINELY RE-TUNE THE PLAN

Actual human capital supply, demand, and gaps are in constant flux. We know that life never follows the expected path, no matter how thorough we plan; rather our plans are more of a guide that illustrate where we would like to end up. Strategic workforce plans must be tuned to account for changes to the demand for talent, the supply of talent, as well as HR, recruiter, and hiring manager feedback.

Strategic planners must work closely with the implementers of their plans. An understanding of the rationale behind the plan and its details can empower hiring managers and recruiters to make the next best worker-type choice when gaps cannot be filled as quickly as expected. Additionally, recruiters and human resource managers may be able to provide ideas on how to design a more achievable plan.

The strategic plan must be monitored routinely and early-warning signals detected so that necessary adjustments can be made quickly. By reviewing the strategic workforce plan regularly, unexpected changes in labor demand and supply can be handled most effectively and a company's potential for profit maximized.

Key Points: Strategic Workforce Planning

- The discipline of strategic workforce planning has rapidly evolved.

- A strategic workforce plan drives the HCSC, so every company needs one. Getting started probably means hiring skill sets from outside of HR.

- A strategic workforce plan must address both the permanent workforce and the flexible workforce at the same time.

- A strategic workforce plan provides an overview of the current workforce, describes how the workforce is changing and what the plan is to solve skill shortages and surpluses.

- The plan needs to be tuned routinely to accommodate changes in demand, supply, and feedback from the plan's implementers (e.g. HR, recruiters, hiring managers).

- No matter whether it is a candidate-rich or candidate-poor market, strengthening relationships with potential future employees is good business.

Chapter 9: Partner with Strategic Human Capital Suppliers

CHAPTER OBJECTIVES:

- Identify common types of human capital suppliers.

- Describe how to transform selected staffing vendors into long-term partners.

- Explain the benefits of creating strategic relationships with suppliers.

HUMAN CAPITAL SUPPLIERS

Our rough estimate is that the U.S. human capital supplier industry alone generates well over one trillion dollars in revenue; it's big business and some of the largest suppliers are Fortune 500 companies, including: Adecco, BearingPoint, IBM, Kelly Services, Manpower, and Robert Half International.

There are a variety of firms that supply human capital to hiring companies:

Staffing firms. Staffing firms employ workers on a temporary basis and place them at client locations. These temp or contingent workers become part of the client workforce but are employed by the staffing firm who marks up the temp's hourly pay rate. Temporary workers have permeated every type of industry, experience level, and job function.

Recruitment agencies. Recruitment agencies find permanent employees for their clients. Hiring companies pay a fee, typically twenty to thirty percent of the candidate's first-year salary.

Executive search firms. Executive search agencies specialize in finding highly paid resources for their clients. Search firms receive a fee for finding the candidate that is eventually hired by the client company. The term "executive" is not consistently defined, but typically refers to positions at the director level up to the CEO, and may even extend to board members. Executive search firm fees are generally equivalent to one year of salary of the position they are searching for and firms are usually hired on a contingent or retained basis. A contingent executive search is one where the search firm gets paid only if they provide the candidate that is eventually hired. Retained search means that the search firm gets paid monthly whether or not they fill the position.

Professional services firms. For our purposes, we define professional services firms as those companies that provide consulting services. In most cases, professional services firms take on the responsibility for delivering specific work products in addition to supplying the team of people required to produce the work. They typically charge for services by the hour (time and materials), by project milestone, or for a fixed fee.

Business services firms. Business services include a wide variety of services provided by outside service firms, e.g. legal, accounting, marketing, IT, cafeteria, facilities, and maintenance. Business services are provided by outside firms that are specialists in their particular area. Some analysts consider staffing, recruitment, and outsourcing services as business services, but we consider those as separate categories.

Business process outsourcers (BPO). This is where professional and business services firms take on responsibility for work products; BPO firms take on the total operations for a portion of an organization, often an entire department. An HR outsourcer (HRO) is an outsourcing firm that takes over all or part of firm's HR organization. A recruitment process outsourcer (RPO) takes over all or part of a firm's staffing and recruiting function. The HRO and RPO industries are a subset of the overarching category, BPO. There is a growing trend to outsource non-core business functions to BPO organizations. A number of staffing and professional services firms have begun to provide outsourcing services. While recruitment and human resources may not be a company's core competency, their workforce is certainly a core component of their enterprise. Because they are deeply integrated into their client's organization, RPOs and HROs have highly strategic supplier relationships.

Each of these human capital supplier types includes specialists and generalists. Specialist firms may focus on a particular industry, skill set, or geography. The largest firms tend to be generalists, serving all of their customer's human capital needs on a worldwide basis. While human capital suppliers tend to focus on one of the six areas above, many follow market needs and crossover, offering a variety of services or even create their own hybrid offerings.

GET TO KNOW YOUR SUPPLIERS

If you conducted the analysis suggested in Chapter 4, "Wrap Your Arms around the Total Cost of Human Capital," you may have been surprised by the vast number of human capital suppliers in your supply chain. In most organizations, a wide variety of staffing vendors are hired by various departments or individual hiring managers and coded in a multitude of ways in the accounting system. These process variances make it difficult to identify all of the current human capital providers. It is difficult to improve supplier processes, relationships, and performance without having a complete understanding of who the human capital vendors are on a worldwide basis. In addition to building a long list of current human capital suppliers, discover as much as possible about the scope of their services, their strengths and weaknesses, the quality and relative cost of their human capital, past performance data, duration of the relationship, amount paid to them each year, and which hiring managers and internal buyers favor them. Locate any existing agreements between the firm and these vendors, and review key terms. Many staffing suppliers utilize sub-vendors, so learn as much as possible about these secondary suppliers to have as much awareness as possible of the total HCSC. By the end of this information gathering exercise, there should be enough information to evaluate the relationship and be very clear about the value each supplier adds to the company's product or service.

TRANSFORMING SUPPLIERS FROM VENDORS INTO PARTNERS

Master supplier manager, Michael Dell, has said to "keep your friends close, and your suppliers closer." In our experience we have found that a number of clients act in exactly the opposite way. They seem to believe that their best vendor-negotiation strategy is to keep suppliers at an arm's length. These hiring companies withhold strategic information, are close-lipped about needs and issues, and are combative to vendors in order to get lower pricing. Leaders such as Dell, Wal-Mart, and Toyota have taught us that there is another, more positive and profitable way to work with suppliers, and that is to partner with them.

Consolidate

One of the keys to developing long-term, strategic partnerships with staffing suppliers is to not have too many. Vendor consolidation has become increasingly common. During a consolidation exercise, rates for specific skill sets are compared to current market rates and can dramatically decrease immediately. Hiring companies who consolidate vendors typically end up with a tiered list of approved vendors. Tier-1 vendors may have the first right of refusal, no right to refuse, or a set time by which they must fill a job order before the order is distributed to tier-2 or tier-3 vendors. A company should not have more than five to eight vendors assigned to each tier. Analyzing existing human capital suppliers on a quarterly basis, reviewing long-term vendor performance, and refreshing pricing and terms with a fewer number of vendors can have a meaningful and positive impact on the cost and quality of the portion of the workforce that is provided by outside suppliers. Establish a process where, based upon quarterly performance, suppliers can move up or down the supply chain tiers.

Develop long-term relationships

With fewer suppliers the firm is better positioned to develop a tight-knit, longer-term relationship. In order to provide the best service, strategic human capital suppliers must be privy to key business strategies and plans. Suppliers can provide critical input into the strategic workforce plan such as current market rates and scarcity of skills. From their neutral, outside perspective they may also be best positioned to provide general information about the labor market.

Long-term relationships allow the two parties to get to know each other's strengths and weaknesses. For decades, supply chain leaders have been "opening the kimono" with strategic suppliers and building a two-way relationship. Once a long-term commitment has been agreed upon, suppliers and hiring companies can share business processes, establish end-to-end metrics, connect their technology, and collaborate to solve problems. This open communication approach has been gaining steam since Toyota and other progressive firms learned that they needed to involve their suppliers in supply chain management principles if they wanted to eliminate waste and maximize efficiency. Hiring companies need to constantly engage with their suppliers and take a deep look into their supplier's operations in order to work together to take cost out of the entire HCSC while improving quality.

Manage supplier performance

Supply chain leaders learned to set four to six key performance indicators for each strategic vendor and communicate supplier performance standards that link to the company's strategy. Suppliers must clearly understand how they add value to the client's product or service. Supplier performance must be measured on a weekly basis and issues discussed. Corrective action plans can then be agreed and tracked.

Supplier dashboards have become a widespread business practice, but if they are not implemented properly, they can be fraught with problems. Sherry Gordon, author of *Supplier Evaluation and Performance Excellence* and Spend Matters' guest blogger, highlights the following twelve common supplier scorecard pitfalls[1]:

1. Firms measure what is easily measured rather than what is important to the business. Too often people come up with a wish list of metrics or KPIs that they would like to use, but end up actually deploying different and less meaningful metrics and KPIs because the data for the desired metrics are not readily available. This can lead to #2.

2. Metrics are borrowed from other companies and are not sufficiently relevant or meaningful to the borrowing firm. While it is helpful to learn what other firms, even in the same industry, are measuring on their scorecards, other firms' metrics may not fit your business, or you may not be able to gather the same data as other firms. Poor fit means poor results.

3. Some firms try to track too many KPIs or measure too many suppliers to be effective. Quality of metrics always trumps quantity.

4. Metrics do not support or are not aligned with a firm's business goals. Supplier scorecards developed in a vacuum without regard to senior management's goals and objectives will have a lower chance of success and of senior management support in the form of resources.

5. Scorecards may lack credibility and transparency and thus can be subject to doubt and dispute, both within a company and with suppliers. Who wants to waste time arguing about whether the numbers are right?

6. Scorecards that require too much data cleansing and manual manipulation to produce have a lower probability of success. The more tweaking required, the greater the amount of additional (scarce) resources that may be needed, which will potentially lower the credibility of the metrics with suppliers.

7. Internal stakeholders don't provide input on a timely basis or not at all. If internal support and discipline is lacking, the best-laid plans for measuring internal stakeholder satisfaction can disappear, derailing your HCSC supplier evaluation process.

8. Scorecard results are not regularly shared with suppliers. If scorecards are kept a secret from suppliers, performance improvement will not result. And, yes, I have seen organizations that don't get around to sharing supplier scorecard results with their suppliers.

9. Suppliers are unclear about their customer's performance expectations. When suppliers are not sure what performance the customer expects, how can they meet customer performance expectations? Result of scorecards: nothing happens.

10. Metrics are confusing or have no meaning to suppliers. Suppliers: Did you ever see mysterious metrics on your scorecard and wonder — where did they come from, what do they mean and, even sometimes, is the customer making them up?

11. There is little or no action or follow-through that results from the scorecards. (i.e., suppliers do not see recognition, rewards, corrective actions, or disengagement as a result of their performance). If there are no consequences or rewards, a supplier will soon realize that scorecards are just customer window dressing. Yep, we've got supplier scorecards, check.

12. Scorecard metrics are simply not actionable. Or, scorecard metrics do not help expose the root causes of problems, making it difficult for the supplier to undertake corrective actions. Without action and results, scorecards can be a waste of resources.

To improve supplier performance, monthly, if not weekly, feedback is essential. This may sound obvious, but staffing suppliers are often starving for direct client feedback. There are a number of causes for the lack of communication. One reason is that hiring companies have not centralized the management of staffing suppliers and have not formalized a staffing supplier relationship management program. Without a central authority responsible for sharing performance results, there is no single party assigned the role, and feedback does not happen. Along these lines, there may be no set performance standards or method for gathering performance data, making feedback loose and subjective rather than continuous and objective. Without automation, and with so many vendors, it may be just too much effort to manually track and communicate supplier performance. While vendor management systems are providing more and more supplier scorecard functionality, they also put technology between the client and supplier, which can make it difficult to have a constructive dialogue about performance issues and corrective actions.

BENEFITS OF STRATEGIC SUPPLIERS

Lower total cost of human capital

Supply chain experts have learned that when companies and suppliers work together to eliminate waste and increase efficiencies, cost can be permanently removed from the entire HCSC. In many cases the costs can be decreased quickly and further reductions continued over the long term. For human capital suppliers, especially for services often viewed as commodity purchases such a temp labor, suppliers are used to continually being pressured to reduce their prices in order to win business. If they don't allow their margins to be squeezed, they can lose out to their competition. If they do reduce their margins, the business may be unprofitable, thus reducing the longer-term viability of the supplier. By making a long-term commitment to key and proven firms, clients can work with suppliers hand in hand to reduce the actual cost of doing business. This approach is beneficial to both the client and the human capital supplier because the total cost of human capital is fundamentally lowered and both parties can maintain profitability.

Faster time to fill

Cost is reduced by removing waste and increasing efficiencies as well as decreasing time to fill. Minimizing the time a requirement is unfilled is critical because, if the position is really needed, the lack of a worker decreases company revenue. While a single open requisition may not have a measurable impact on revenue, a consistent pattern of long fill times will certainly have a notable reduction on the hiring company's potential revenue. Time to fill can be increased in a number of ways. Supply chain gurus have shown us that sharing monthly and weekly planning data with suppliers certainly enables them to proactively have human capital available just in time. We have also seen companies integrate directly into their supplier's technology so there is no delay in exchanging information about open orders. Supplier relationship management programs provide a myriad of opportunities to decrease the time to fill.

Higher quality workforce

By communicating clear performance requirements and sharing weekly feedback about opportunities to improve, suppliers will provide higher quality and better-fit resources over time. Worker quality is difficult to measure and forecast. Strategic suppliers who hone their assessment and selection processes to better align with their client's needs and culture over time are best positioned to consistently deliver the right talent, at the right time, and at the right price.

- Get to know all of your human capital vendors and be clear about the value each supplier provides the organization.

- Margin squeezing is a short-sighted approach and a good way to put suppliers out of business. Work with strategic suppliers to eliminate wasteful activities, streamline processes, and reduce the cost of the entire staffing and recruitment process.

- Scorecards are a great way to track and manage supplier performance as long as the metrics tie into the company's goals.

- Strategic supplier relationships decrease the total cost of human capital, decrease time to fill, and improve the quality of the workforce, which results in higher profits.

Chapter 10: Five Ways to Get Started

CHAPTER OBJECTIVES:

- Explain the importance of establishing a governance structure before launching a human capital supply chain.

- Describe how to develop a multi-year roadmap of human capital supply chain projects.

- Share tried-and-true approaches to getting a human capital supply chain off the ground.

After reading the previous nine chapters of this book, the idea of beginning to establish and manage a corporation's HCSC may seem like a daunting task. Based on decades of enterprise program and project management experience we suggest putting a few fundamentals in place before starting.

The two most important fundamentals are the HCSC governance structure and the roadmap. The governance structure identifies the business owners of the HCSC and establishes the chain of command for decision-making and issue resolution. The roadmap describes the goals and timing of key projects and includes as much supporting detail as possible. The best starter projects are low risk, low investment, and proven ideas. The last section of the chapter provides five common ways that other companies have kicked-off their HCSC management programs.

ESTABLISH GOVERNANCE

If there is one thing we have learned through the school of project management hard knocks, it is the importance of establishing a governance structure with defining roles and responsibilities before the program of work starts. Often organizations are uncomfortable setting up this kind of chain of command, especially organizations that have consensus management philosophies and informal business cultures. Be assured: when the project gets tough, you'll be grateful to have a governance structure to fall back on.

Governance structures are often used to accelerate project progress, establish review and sign-off hierarchy for key deliverables, escalate and resolve issues, and manage scope changes. Governance structures need to be used throughout the project, especially *before* there is a problem. If everyone in the chain of command gets practice acting in their assigned role and understands how approvals and escalations will be handled, the project team can more effectively and efficiently handle issues as they arise.

It is important to consider all the various stakeholder groups when setting up a HCSC governance structure. Review Chapter 5 "Engage the Stakeholders" to ensure that all of the necessary roles and organizations, especially the CEO, are included. It is important to include representatives from HR and procurement at each level of the governance structure and to include subject matter experts (SMEs) who understand the strategy and business process for each worker type. Each of these stakeholders is responsible for optimizing the company's workforce in some way, but in many companies this will be the first time they have been organized and working together as a team.

Executive Sponsor

Role:

- Evangelizes HCSC concepts, and communicates the strategy, plan, and progress to internal and external parties;

- Funds the project;

- Reviews project and program status monthly and removes roadblocks as needed; and

- Reviews project outcomes but is unlikely to review lower-level work products.

Ideal Characteristics:

- CEO;

- Understands the importance of the workforce to the company's success and competitive advantage; and

- Has the respect of HR, procurement, and line management.

Project Sponsor

Role:

- Responsible for monitoring project and program progress with a focus on high-level monthly outcomes (e.g. meeting the budget and delivering the expected benefits);

- Signs-off on key project deliverables;

- Makes key decisions, resolves escalated issues and mitigates project risks; and

- Identifies key decisions and issues for escalation to the executive sponsor.

Ideal Characteristics:

- CFO or VP level resource;

- Track record of success running large projects and programs;

- Appreciates HCSC concepts and understands the high-level costs and benefits; and

- Supports the project owner and is able to help navigate the organization and remove roadblocks.

Project Owner

Role:

- Accountable for program and project success and ensures project objectives are met;

- Proactively drives projects to plan on a day-to-day basis;

- Identifies, mitigates, communicates, and escalates project issues and risks;

- Ensures a high-quality analysis of issues and opportunities is conducted for robust project definition, planning and execution;

- Reviews and reports program status weekly; and

- Ensures governance structure is followed.

Ideal Characteristics:

- Director level resource;
- Takes personal accountability for project outcomes, a driving personality not just a project status tracker;
- Passionate about HCSC concepts;
- Understands the holistic business process, including business planning, workforce planning, staffing, and recruitment;
- Understands how each worker type strategically benefits the company;
- Experienced and skilled cross-functional facilitator and program manager;
- Good communicator and well networked across the organization; and
- Available and committed to the project on a full-time basis.

Subject Matter Expert

Role:

- Represents their department and/or area of expertise;
- Understands and explains the key aspects of their current and desired business process as needed;
- Helps to brainstorm, prioritize, and develop HCSC improvement ideas; and
- Helps to identify project issues and risks.

Ideal Characteristics:

- Highly experienced resources who understand the ins and outs of the area of expertise;

- Good communicators who appreciate the opportunity to be part of a wider team;

- Strategic thinkers who want to improve overall company performance, not just improve their area of focus; and

- Highly regarded throughout the organization and embraces change.

The project owner may have supporting staff. For the sake of the governance chart, these resources report into the project owner and are not directly included in the chain of command. Because these resources are very involved in the project, they could be shown on the governance chart, in a separate box to the side of the project owner.

The two most important individuals in the governance structure are the project owner and the executive sponsor. It is absolutely essential that the project owner feels a personal sense of ownership over the success of the project throughout the company. Project owners that define their role narrowly and focus on tracking rather than driving the schedule, budget, and project outcomes will have difficulty keeping forward momentum on a HCSC project that is strategic and cross-functional in nature. The executive sponsor must also be personally committed to and engaged with HCSC concepts. The executive sponsor is "the face" of the project, communicating and selling the project's purpose and benefits to the entire company.

Define Your Human Capital Supply Chain

Discover

Before getting started on improving a HCSC, gather as much information about the current situation and strategy goals as possible. After conducting this research, you have a holistic view of the stakeholders, worker types, business processes, technologies, and key staffing suppliers involved. In addition to capturing the current state of affairs, gather historical perspectives, including past mistakes and the rationale that drives the current situation, wish-list items, and initiatives that are currently underway.

Develop

Define existing business processes (See Chapter 8). It is important to understand which departments and stakeholders are responsible for each process step and how the processes vary across worker types. Don't be surprised to find wide fluctuations with similar processes across the organization. One of the goals of a HCSCM program is to unify the business processes. Leveraging the same business processes nationally and globally will reduce the cost of human capital management and may also allow for more proactive management of the mix of human capital used. In order to align business processes, first understand how they currently function.

Dive into greater detail and describe the contribution and costs of each worker type to the organization, especially if different organizations are responsible for different worker types. Gather data around the numbers and costs of workers in each type. Are the sizes, quality, and costs of each worker-type group managed deliberately or is the resulting workforce the outcome of tactical decision-making?

Include a narrative that describes how well stakeholder groups interact with HR, procurement, and line management. Do they have a high level or deep understanding of each other's business processes? How well do all the groups work together? Do they understand the strengths and weaknesses of each skill set? Does management swap resources between the groups to develop a shared language, set of goals, and business process?

Another main area of focus is the key metrics and performance data. It is important to understand which performance data is currently available, tracked, and managed. Successful supply chain management depends on frequent routine measurement and reporting of business process performance. Companies should also describe the key performance indicators that they would like to track on an ongoing basis. Both current and desired performance measures and data should be described.

Describing current and desired HCSC processes, stakeholders, and metrics, is in effect, defining the human capital supply chain, and this critical and compulsory step is conducted early on in any HCSCM program.

Identify Pain Points and Opportunities

Now that we have a clear picture of the current and potential HCSC, we can begin reviewing and analyzing each component to identify pain points and opportunities for improvement. (See Chapter 2 for traditional supply chain tools, e.g. identifying waste, root cause analysis, continuous improvement that can be applied.)

Providing detailed descriptions of each problem area or opportunity, especially information around the cause, frequency, impact, and likelihood of the problem will help identify the most critical issues. While companies may be practiced at identifying organizational, process, and technology gaps, it is helpful to identify data and reporting gaps as well as strategies and plans that need development. For all of these areas, consider each and every worker type. Lastly, analyze the HCSC holistically and globally for additional issues and opportunities.

Since pain points and opportunities will change over time, the first list of improvements will be the hardest to create. As you become experienced at managing a HCSC, you will identify new issues and more opportunities. Formally revise the issues and opportunities list at least once each year.

DESIGN SOLUTIONS AND PROJECTS

For each problem area or opportunity, brainstorm multiple solution approaches. Solutions may include a combination of process, procedure, organization, technology, or other changes. Each solution approach needs to be described, because the effort and cost of each approach is important information, as is the level of risk. Dependencies between solution approaches must also be identified and any key elements of timing made known. In the end, you want a complete profile of each solution approach. If there is more than one feasible approach impacting the same component of the HCSC, rank them.

Create A Roadmap

Once a list of developed improvement ideas is made, prioritize them and define them as implementation projects. Develop and document the prioritization criteria and evaluate each project idea. Most companies prioritize the lowest-risk, fastest-ROI projects first. Complex or cross-functional projects or those with many dependencies will be implemented after there have been some program successes.

The last piece of data needed is a feel for how much change the company can tolerate at any one time and how much investment they can afford to budget for HCSC initiatives. This information, along with the prioritized projects, allows you to overlay projects on a high-level timeline. Keep the roadmap timing pretty high-level and provide the most detail around near-term plans. The first year of a roadmap may provide a breakdown of projects by month, year two may describe project plans by quarter, and year three may not require any timing expectation. For most industries, a three-year roadmap is sufficient; longer-term strategies and plans can be described using prose and added to the roadmap in the future.

If a company is committed to actively managing a HCSC, the improvement efforts will be ongoing. This means there will be a stream of projects that are executed over a number of years. This web of related projects, also known as a program of work, overlaid on a high-level timeline, is what we call a human capital supply chain roadmap.

Write It Down

While it can be time consuming and tedious, it is critical to document your findings in detail and have them reviewed and approved by the members on the HCSC governance chart. This document serves as an introduction to the company's HCSC for both stakeholders and new team members. It also serves as the official record of the starting point and the desired destination. Later on in the project, check in and verify that the company is still aligned with the initial focus, and on track with the original goals. In some cases, you'll recall important ideas that were inadvertently dropped. In other cases, you'll want to amend the document to reflect what you've learned along the way.

Documents like this lose their value if they are not kept current. They are highly valuable to the organization, and remain so over time when they are reviewed and updated on a regular basis. Quarterly updates will ensure that the document evolves along with the HCSC program.

FIVE WAYS TO GET STARTED: IDEAS FOR YOUR FIRST PROJECT

Case studies and leading HCSC implementers suggest the most common approaches to getting a HCSCM program off the ground:

1. **Determine the total cost of human capital (top-down and/or bottom-up approaches)**

   HR and procurement departments have wanted to increase their corporate profile for decades. If CEOs understood how much they are actually spending on their total workforce (i.e. across all worker types) they would be more attentive to workforce management issues. (Chapter 4 describes how companies can deepen their understanding of the total cost of their complete workforce and explores top-down and bottom-up approaches.) There are a number of consulting firms who have experience gathering the necessary financial data and comparing it against benchmarking data.

2. **Consolidate staffing suppliers and identify potential strategic partners**

   Optimizing staffing suppliers has proven to reduce the cost of human capital and, when implemented well, increase workforce quality and productivity. Establishing strategic supplier relationships has been a proven manufacturing and distribution supply chain practice (see Chapter 9). Consolidating suppliers takes management attention but very little investment, and there is virtually no risk. Many firms have kicked off their HCSCM programs with a staffing supplier consolidation project.

3. **Implement VMS technology**

Since the '90s, hundreds of companies have successfully implemented VMS technology and derived substantial benefits and cost savings post-implementation. Unlike other areas of technology that require large up-front financial investments, VMS programs are almost always supplier funded. That means that hiring companies can increase their visibility into the cost of their flexible workforce without much effort.

4. **Develop a strategic workforce plan**

It is critical, especially for knowledge- or service-based companies, that business planning be more tightly tied to staffing and recruitment. Just as manufacturing companies tied business forecasting to production planning, and retail companies tied consumer sales to distribution, knowledge-based companies need to tie business performance to staffing and recruitment on a real-time basis. Developing a strategic workforce plan is a low-cost, low-risk first step (see Chapter 8).

5. **Focus on a high-impact worker type**

Another approach to getting your HCSCM program off the ground is to identify the largest, unmanaged worker type (a.k.a. labor-based category) and focus on improving that particular segment of the workforce. Conduct a focused analysis and develop a highly detailed improvement plan or program, which takes cost out of the process and improves quality and productivity for a single worker type.

- Develop a solid and cross-functional HCSCM governance structure before starting a program of work.

- The two most important people in the governance structure are the project owner the executive sponsor.

- The ideal project owner is one who shows a great deal of personal ownership and accountability for project outcomes and is able to foster the engagement of HR, procurement, and management stakeholders.

- The ideal executive sponsor is one who is deeply engaged with HCSC concepts and communicates the merits of the project to the entire company.

- Documenting the current HCSC situation and plans may be tedious and time consuming, but it is a valuable asset and training tool.

- Develop a roadmap that outlines two to three years of planned projects, and include as much supporting detail as possible.

- Plan on updating your HCSC roadmap routinely; don't let it get out of date.

- There are many ways to get started on your HCSCM program of work. If you stick to the well-traveled road, you are sure to show cost savings along with workforce quality and productivity improvements early on, which will help increase buy-in and momentum for the program.

References

CHAPTER 2
THIRTY YEARS OF MANUFACTURING SUPPLY CHAIN EXPERIENCE

[1] Hugos, M. (2006, 2nd Edition). *Essentials of Supply Chain Management.* Hoboken, New Jersey: John Wiley & Sons, Inc., p. 3.

[2] Ibid.

[3] Anderson, D. L., Britt, F. F., and Favre, D. J. (2007, April 1). "The 7 Principles of Supply Chain Management." Retrieved March 29, 2009, from *Supply Chain Management Review*: http://www.scmr.com/article/CA6432096.html

[4] Hugos, M. (2006, 2nd Edition). *Essentials of Supply Chain Management.* Hoboken, New Jersey: John Wiley & Sons, Inc., p. 2.

[5] Wailgum, T. and Worthen, B. (updated 2008, November 20). "Supply Chain Management Definition and Solutions." Retrieved March 29, 2009, from *CIO.com* http://www.cio.com/article/40940/Supply_Chain_Management_Definition_and_Solutions

[6] Ibid.

[7] Blanchard, D. (2008, May 30). "The Top 25 Supply Chains of

2008." Retrieved March 29, 2009, from *IndustryWeek* http://
forums.industryweek.com/showthread.php?t=1684

[8] Hugos, M. (2006, 2nd Edition). *Essentials of Supply Chain
Management.* Hoboken, New Jersey: John Wiley & Sons, Inc.,
p. 5.

[9] Ibid.

[10] Oliver, K., Shorten, D., & Engel, H. (2004, Fall). *Supply
Chain Strategy: Back to Basics.* Retrieved May 9, 2009, from:
http://www.strategy-business.com/press/16635507/04313

CHAPTER 5
ENGAGE THE STAKEHOLDERS

[1] Leibs, S. (2009, February 1). "Soft is Hard" Retrieved April
28, 2009, from *CFO Magazine*: http://www.cfo.com/article.
cfm/13009025?f=related

[2] "Contingent Metrics You Need to Know", *Contingent
Workforce Strategies*, September 2008 Issue: http://
www.staffingindustry.com/Media/ PublishingTitles/
cwsbench0809.pdf

CHAPTER 9
PARTNER WITH STRATEGIC HUMAN CAPITAL SUPPLIERS

[1] Gordon, S. (2009, May 21). "12 Reasons Why Supplier
Scorecards Fail." Retrieved July 6, 2009, from *Spend Matters*:
http://www. spendmatters.com/index.cfm/2009/5/21/12-
Reasons-Why-Supplier- Scorecards-Fail

Resources

INDUSTRY ASSOCIATIONS

American Productivity and Quality Center (APQC)
www.apqc.org

American Staffing Association (ASA)
www.americanstaffing.net

Institute for Supply Management (ISM)
www.ism.ws

International Association for Human Resource Management
(IHRIM)
www.ihrim.org

Society of Human Resource Management (SHRM)
www.shrm.org

Staffing Industry Analysts (SIA)
www.staffingindustry.com

Staffing.org
www.staffing.org

Helpful HR Sites

Electronic Recruiting Exchange (ERE)
www.ere.net

Human Capital Institute
www.humancapitalinstitute.org

Human Resource Executive
www.hrexecutive.com

Human Resources Magazine
www.humanresourcesmagazine.com

Kennedy Information
www.kennedyinfo.com

Taleo Research
http://www.taleo.com/research/research.php

Workforce Magazine
www.workforce.com

Helpful Procurement and Supply Chain Sites

CFO Magazine
www.cfo.com

Harvard Business Review
www.harvardbusiness.org

IndustryWeek
www.industryweek.com

Supply and Demand Chain News
www.sdexec.com

Supply Chain Brain
www.supplychainbrain.com

Selected List of Industry Analysts and Consultants with Human Capital and Supply Chain Practices

Aberdeen Group
www.aberdeen.com

Accenture
www.accenture.com

AMR
www.amrresearch.com

BearingPoint
www.bearingpoint.com

Booz
www.booz.com

The Code Works Inc.
www.thecodeworksinc.com

Deloitte & Touche
www.deloitte.com

Forrester Research
www.forrester.com

Gartner
www.gartner.com

IBM
www.ibm.com

IDC
www.idc.com

Mercer
www.mercer.com

Acronyms

AESC	Association of Executive Search Consultants
AP	Accounts Payable
APQC	American Productivity and Quality Center
AR	Accounts Receivable
ASA	American Staffing Association
ATS	Applicant Tracking System
BI	Business Intelligence
BLS	Bureau of Labor Statistics
BNA	Bureau of National Affairs
BPO	Business Process Outsourcing
CAPS	Center for Advanced Procurement Studies
CEO	Chief Executive Officer
CFO	Chief Financial Officer
COO	Chief Operating Officer

EADG	Employers Association Development Group
EEOC	Equal Employment Opportunity Commission
ERP	Enterprise Resource Planning
FO	Front Office
HC	Human Capital
HCM	Human Capital Management
HCSC	Human Capital Supply Chain
HCSCM	Human Capital Supply Chain Management
HR	Human Resources
HRIS	Human Resource Information System
HRMS	Human Resource Management System
HRO	HR Outsourcer
IPMA-HR	International Public Management Association for Human Resources
IOMA	Institute of Management and Administration, Inc.
ISO	International Organization for Standardization
IT	Information Technology
JIT	Just in Time
KPI	Key Performance Indicator
MSP	Managed Service Program

MV	Master Vendor
NACCB	National Association of Computer Consultant Businesses
OFCCP	Office of Federal Contract Compliance Programs
OSBC	Open Standards Benchmarking Collaborative
PEO	Professional Employment Organization
PSA	Professional Services Automation
RDCEO	Reusable Definition of Competency or Educational Objective
RFx	Request for information, proposal, or quote
RMS	Recruitment Management System
ROI	Return on Investment
RPO	Recruitment Process Outsourcing
SaaS	Software as a Service
SCM	Supply Chain Management
SCOR	Supply Chain Operations Reference Model
SIA	Staffing Industry Analysts
SIBC	Staffing Industry Benchmarking Consortium
SKU	Stock Keeping Unit
SLA	Service Level Agreement
SME	Subject Matter Expert

SOA	Service Oriented Architecture
SOW	Statement of Work
SRM	Supplier Relationship Management
TAS	Talent Acquisition System
TMS	Talent Management Suite
TQM	Total Quality Management
VMS	Vendor Management System
XML	Extensible Markup Language

Glossary

80/20 rule. A rule based on Pareto principle used to describe phenomenon in which 80 percent of variations observed can be explained by 20 percent of the causes of that variation.

Benchmark. Metric used to measure, assess, and evaluate activities and performance; crucial to understanding operational health and identifying opportunities for improvement.

Business planning. The process of identifying and defining business goals and objectives, and the strategy to achieve the goals.

Business process outsourcing. BPO involves contracting of a specific business functions, processes or tasks (such as recruitment, payroll processing, and customer service) to a third-party service provider so that the company can focus its resources on core activities critical to growth. BPO service providers have over time built expertise and efficiencies that provide cost savings to their clients and reduce the time to market for new and expanding businesses.

Business services provider. Niche experts such as attorneys, accountants, marketing and PR professionals, etc., who provide services on an hourly, retainer, or project basis to an organization.

Category. Term used by procurement to describe a type, of expense, such as temporary services, professional services, marketing, cafeteria services, or office supplier.

Consultant. An expert or professional with knowledge in a specific area (management, accountancy, technology, finance, marketing, etc.) and provides advice to clients in the area of expertise.

Contingent labor. Those who work for an employer for a specific (limited) duration and are not entitled to employer benefits and employment protection; includes temp workers, independent contractors and consultants, interns, etc.; used to meet seasonal or unexpected demand and reduce training and benefit components of their labor costs.

Contract-to-hire. Circumstance in which a hiring decision is made during or after the temp employee has completed an assignment.

Contractor. A person or organization hired to deliver specific services, tasks, or activities as defined in the terms and conditions laid out in a contract.

Corp-to-corp. Human capital is procured from an external corporation such as an S corporation, C corporation, LLC, or Limited Partnership.

Direct employee. Employee hired to work on a regular basis full-time or part-time on employer's premises or other designated location, and is provided with regular pay, employer benefits, and employment protection.

Enterprise resource planning. A single system (or multiple modules of a system) implemented across departments to integrate all business functions, supported by a single database. ERP systems typically handle end-to-end business functions such as manufacturing, logistics, production, inventory, shipping, distribution, invoicing and billing, finance and accounting, human resources.

Fishbone diagram. Also known as cause-and-effect diagram, developed by Kaoru Ishikawa as a quality improvement tool used to understand the effect and possible causes of an effect in a process or system.

Flexible workforce. A generic term that implies the use of non-traditional employment arrangements, such as temp employees, contractors, seasonal hires, or interns hired to meet short-term needs for specific duration.

Governance structure. Tool used to describe roles and responsibilities of various stakeholders to ensure appropriate flow of information, resolution of issues, and chain of command.

Holistic. A comprehensive view of an organization, including its people, processes, and systems.

Human capital. Skills and knowledge workers have or acquire during a job that increase the employee's value.

Human capital supply chain. Business processes, technology, and organizations responsible for planning, hiring, onboarding, and offboarding a company's human capital. Human capital supply chains link business strategy, business performance, strategic workforce planning, and staffing for improved corporate financial management and greater business success.

Human capital supply chain management. Planning, scheduling, and controlling business processes, technology, and organizations in the human capital supply chain in order to ensure the right talent is in the right place, at the right price, and at the right time.

Human resource outsourcing. Paying an outside individual or company for HR activities such as recruiting, payroll, benefits administration.

Independent contractor. Self-employed or freelance workers who provide specific services for a defined time period (as determined in a contract); may be hired to do similar tasks as employees, but employers do not generally withhold payroll taxes.

ISO. International Organization for Standardization is the primary developer and publisher of international standards and provides requirements and gives guidance on good management practices. The standard provides a framework for taking a systematic approach to managing the organization's processes so that it is possible to consistently turn out product that satisfies customers' expectations.

Just in time. Manufacturing strategy (also known as JIT, Kanban, Toyota Production System, Lean Manufacturing) first adopted by Toyota to improve quality and productivity by eliminating inventory and idle time by aligning production to market needs and demands. JIT manufacturing means that the right product is produced and delivered to the consumer at the right time and at the right cost and price. JIT allows organizations to cost-efficiently respond to market demand regardless of the level of demand.

Key performance indicators. Financial and non-financial measures that provide high-level snapshot of an organization's health; used to evaluate and assess the overall performance of the organization.

Labor-based category. Term used by procurement to describe services expenses, e.g. temporary services, professional services, marketing, cafeteria services, and non-goods-related expenses e.g. office supplies.

Offboarding. Encompasses tasks and requirements associated with employee termination; functions typically include forms management, exit interviews, and security deactivation and IT system retrieval, termination benefits enrollment, outplacement services, etc.

Onboarding. Encompasses tasks and requirements involved with acclimating and engaging a new employee; functions typically include: forms and task management, new employee orientation and training, benefits enrollment, IT and physical access, equipment and space allocation, and social assimilation.

Outsourcer. An organization that subcontracts a business function, process, or tasks to a third party.

Pain point. Term used to describe challenges or operational or system inefficiencies that prevent a business from effectively achieving its objectives.

Pareto chart. Vertical bar chart that presents values in descending order of frequency to depict most significant element or situation; widely used as a problem-solving and quality improvement technique by prioritizing causes of a problem.

Performance management. Process of setting goals and objectives, and measuring performance against those goals; can apply to performance of an organization, departments, processes, employees, etc.; includes activities to ensure that defined goals are consistently met in an effective and efficient manner.

Performance metrics. Financial and non-financial measures used to assess performance of an organization, department, processes, employees, etc.

Permanent workforce. An organization's full-time and part-time employees.

Procurement. A department in an organization that buys goods and services for the organization.

Professional employment organization (PEO). Employer of record on employees W-2, providing human resources, employee benefits, payroll, workers compensation, and outsourcing services through a co-employment model, and the client organization directs employee's day-to-day activities and duties.

Program of work. Group of related projects that deliver business value when implemented.

Recession. National Bureau of Economic research defines recession as a significant decline in economic activity spread across the economy normally visible in real GDP, real income, employment, industrial production, and wholesale-retail sales.

Recruiting. Process of sourcing, identifying, screening, and hiring a candidate for a particular position or job assignment.

Recruitment process outsourcing. Relationship in which a third-party firm is contracted to staff and manage all or part of internal recruiting functions.

Return on Investment (ROI). A measure of a company's or a project's profitability; used to evaluate the efficiency of an investment. A positive ROI indicates that the project saves money or time.

Roadmap. Plan that provides clear objectives, and the strategy and actions required for achieving the objectives.

Root cause analysis. Technique used to resolve problems by identifying the underlying origins of the problem.

Silo. Business environment characterized by lack of communication and common goals between the departments in an organization (or organizations in a supply chain). In a silo environment, businesses are unable to take advantage of information residing within the organization because of lack of communication.

Six Sigma. Quality improvement initiative initially implemented by Motorola to reduce number of defects by identifying and removing the cause of defects and variation in manufacturing and business processes. A business is considered to have Six Sigma level of quality standards, when there are only 3.4 defects per million output.

Sourcing. Process of finding, assessing, and procuring goods and/or services.

Spend. Expenses incurred by an organization to procure goods and services for the organization. Spend categories include print, travel, telecommunication, contract labor, office supplies, outsourced services, etc.

Staffing. Process of filling an open position by hiring a new employee (temp or permanent) or by re-assigning existing employees.

Staffing supplier. Organization that provides staffing services by assisting clients in filling open positions with temp, contract, or contract-to-hire employees.

Stakeholder. Person, group, or organization that can directly or indirectly affect or can be affected (gain or lose) by the actions of an organization.

Strategic supplier. Person or company an organization has a negotiated contract with to deliver goods or services over the term of the agreement, but under predetermined terms and conditions basically to obtain time and cost efficiencies.

Strategic workforce plan. Plan used to identify staffing levels required to meet business objectives and describe the process to achieve the required staffing level, involving tasks such as workforce forecasting, workforce gap analysis, workforce supply and demand analysis, workforce monitoring, etc.

Supply chain management. Planning, scheduling, and controlling business processes, technology, and organizations in the supply chain in order to ensure the right product or service is delivered in the right place, at the right price, and at the right time.

Talent acquisition. Process of sourcing, selecting, and hiring various worker types (temporary, permanent, contract, etc) with special skills, experience, and knowledge to derive competitive advantage.

Talent management. Encompasses talent acquisition activities to develop and retain employees in an organization; includes recruitment, retention, training and development, performance management, and workforce planning.

Talent mix. The combination of worker types (temporary, permanent, contract, skilled, unskilled) that delivers the best value to the company.

Temporary worker. Employee hired usually through a staffing firm to perform tasks or provide services for a definite time period ranging from a few hours to a few years. The staffing firm is the employer-of-record, and generates the W-2s.

Tier 2 VMS vendors. The sub-vendors (secondary suppliers) to whom a job order is distributed when the Tier 1 vendors (preferred vendors) fail to fill the order. Tier 1 vendors are typically given forty-eight hours to fill a job requisition after which the requisition is distributed to Tier 2 vendors.

Tier 2 ERP vendors. Vendors not considered the market leaders but have perfectly sufficient functionality and cost less.

Total cost of human capital. All expenses incurred by an organization to acquire and manage its workforce.

Total quality management. Philosophies and methodologies adopted by many supply chain management programs to continually remove product defects by systematically identifying and addressing inefficiencies and customer service issues.

Vendor management system (VMS). Vendor management system is a web-based system that automates all key aspects of the procurement of staffing services. VMS enables hiring companies to electronically distribute job orders to multiple staffing suppliers for fulfillment.

Waste. Defects and non-value-adding materials, products, activities, and processes.

Worker type. Category such as temporary employee, permanent employee, full-time employee, part-time employee, intern, contractor, consultant, etc.

Workforce. All workers (and worker types) employed by an organization.

Workforce forecasting. Process of predicting the supply and demand of workers in terms of numbers, skills, and types.

Acknowledgements

Our thanks to the many practitioners who reviewed an early copy of the book and provided their thoughts, and to the staff at Mill City Press.

Tim Giehll adds:

Thanks to my executives and board of directors for listening to my Human Capital Supply Chain ideas and incorporating them into Bond's product roadmap and vision for the future. Special thanks to my wife and 3 daughters, who inspire me every day.

Sara Moss adds:

Thanks to my business partner, Jonathan Novich, for his never-ending support and encouragement, and Deepika Kharbanda for her research and analysis support, and Jeff Reeder for encouraging me to be a writer.

About the Authors

TIM GIEHLL

Tim Giehll (tgiehll@eempact.com) is a staffing industry veteran, technology visionary, and manufacturing expert of more than thirty years. He has served for more than a decade as U.S. CEO of Bond Talent & Bond eEmpACT software (a Bond International Software Company), where he has worked with hundreds of temporary staffing firms to automate their operations.

Giehll developed his understanding of complex software environments during the 1990s as CFO for world-renowned supercomputer designer Steve Chen during their $150-million technology venture with IBM and Sequent Computers. He worked in the '80s as a manufacturing accounting manager with Control Data. After meeting with industry visionary Edward Deming in the early '80s, Giehll was instrumental in launching Control Data's world-class manufacturing initiatives, especially just-in-time inventory processes.

In Human Capital Supply Chains, Tim has merged his technology and manufacturing insights to help usher in a new age of global Human Capital Management.

SARA MOSS

Sara Moss (smoss@thecodeworksinc.com) is co-founder and CEO of The Code Works Inc., a technology consulting company focused on the staffing and recruitment industry. She and her team develop actionable technology strategies to enable their clients' business goals.

Moss is a recognized expert in staffing processes and technologies. Her articles and presentations cover a broad range of topics, including human capital procurement, candidate relationship management, job marketing, onboarding, staffing vendor management, and staffing software trends.

Moss was first trained in Total Quality Management (TQM) principles and practices in the early 1990s at US WEST and Accenture. For the first decade of her career, she applied TQM concepts to telecommunications engineering processes for Global 1000 companies and witnessed the resulting benefits.

In *Human Capital Supply Chains*, Sara has translated her engineering experience into hiring and human capital management processes to help corporations dramatically improve their business performance.